TENTACLES..
The Entanglement of Alcoholism

S. Thomas Greeley

TENTACLES.. The Entanglement of Alcoholism
S. Thomas Greeley

Published by
The Cheshire Press
A Division of The Cheshire Group, Inc
PO Box 2090
Andover, MA 01810-0037
www.cheshirepress.com

All rights reserved. No part of this book may be reproduced or transmitted in any form or by any means without the express written consent of the author, except for the inclusion of quotations in reviews.

Copyright © 2014 by S. Thomas Greeley

ISBN: 978-0-9960210-0-5

Library of Congress Control Number: 2014935707

Printed in the United States of America

Any resemblance to individuals or occupations are purely coincidental. All trademarks used herein are for identification only and are used without intent to infringe on the owner's trademarks or other property rights.

Cover layout and illustration Crispin Wood

Greeley, S. Thomas
Tentacles.. The Entanglement of Alcoholism

To my blended Family
Judy, Gwendolyn, Kj, and Christopher
Who gave my Family unexpected love and friendship
Just when we needed it most

THE TRUTH ~

This is a story based on facts that only I can tell through my experience. It is purely truth as I see it. I am writing about a moment in time. It was a time that lasted over 13 years with an alcoholic. A time that I had to learn what was reality, and what was really the pink elephant in the room. It took me more than 13 years to begin to write my story, because I saw myself through the eyes of the alcoholic. I tried to live up to her distorted views or I tried to distort who I was in order to protect my family from the outside world. It was my way of deflecting the truth that was always trying to bore its way into disrupting our lie. No one would have to know the real danger my family was in, because I could handle whatever came my way. I was the martyr, the savior, the gallant knight, the clown that could hang upside down, the good husband, the fun father, the breadwinner, and the "every man". I could do it all, but could never do enough. I was looked up to and ridiculed all at once. My goal was to save my family from a disease that had no conscience, and held us all captive. The harder I fought, the more ground I lost. I wanted the light of truth, but often I found myself hiding in my house from the outside world that would eventually come knocking. I had to keep fighting an invisible foe, one that was relentless in trying to hurt and dismember my heart and soul. I looked for help from my family and friends, but they had no answers. Often they would try reason, but that only works with reasonable people. There is no cause that turns on the disease of alcoholism. There is no controlling it. No creative thinking can out smart it or cure it. Angry words that may be used to guilt or wound, and even brute force, cannot move the alcoholic into taking positive action. In the end I learned that there is nothing "to" fight, because the disease is nothing more than a ghost. I found that the only way to protect myself was through the Al-Anon 12-step program, and the way I found myself there is a story to be told later. Now is the time to tell my story through my experience, strength, and hope.

IN THE BEGINNING

My romance with Lisa began by way of an insurance client of mine who fixed us up. Lisa had recently started working for Bill at a water testing company he owned out in Leominster, Massachusetts. He thought we would be perfect for each other. Her beautiful smile immediately attracted me to her. She was short like me and had long wavy hair. On our first date we did nothing but laugh at each other's lame jokes. I think we both had come off two bad relationships. It felt so different than the way my first wife Mary had made me feel. Mary was sullen, and negative. We had dated from my senior year at the University of Massachusetts into the beginnings of my insurance career, but our marriage began falling apart almost as soon as it began. I knew we were in trouble when I made the comment to her, "We can never have kids, because you're an asshole!" Fortunately she put an end to our misery when she went on a company business trip to Florida and let her guard down, as well as some guy's pants. Upon arriving back to Logan Airport in Boston, she could not look me in the eyes. I thought she was mad that I had not gone with her, but instead it was nothing more than guilt. We tried a short period of marriage counseling, but I knew there was nothing left in my heart. It was time to call it quits. I moved out and into my grandparents' home in Framingham, Massachusetts, since they were living in a nearby nursing home, and I set up my new life there.

I lived with an older college student to whom my grandparents had been renting a room in their downstairs bedroom for $30 per month. He was quiet and odd, but at least I was not alone. My friends tried to fix me up with women, and I tried a long distance relationship with a nice lady whom I had met on a company trip to Milwaukee. But it was too soon. I was caught in between the loss in my heart and the confusion of trying to start over.

After about 6 months, in November of 1987, Bill asked me to come to his company to review the life insurance plan we had in place for his key executives. When I arrived he had me walk around the science lab where they were testing samples of water. There in the lab was this young smiling cutie wearing a white lab coat. Bill introduced us, but a few minutes later in his office he asked me, "What do you think of her?" I said that she seemed nice, but nothing more than that. I was preoccupied with other women that I might have the opportunity to get to know better.

The next day Bill called me and told me that Lisa really liked me and that I should ask her out. I really did not feel any sparks flying between us, but I told him that I would ask her out just to see where this might go. That afternoon I called her at her other part time job at another water testing lab in New Hampshire. When she answered the phone I said, "Guess who?" She replied, "Mark?" I did not know what to say back accept to nervously laugh, and say, "No, this is Tom. The guy you met at Bill's lab the other day?" She acknowledged that she knew who I was. I asked her if she would like to go out with me. She was not sure what her plans were, but she would call me later that night. This all seemed very strange. If this girl was gaga over me, then why did she say another man's name and not mine! I was not sure if this date was going to happen. I had another party to go to in Boston, so if she did not call back I would be fine. I waited a few hours for her call, and finally thought that if she did not call in the next 5 minutes I was going out. Just as I was putting on my jacket and turning the front door knob the phone rang. It was her. I was thrilled. We made a date for the upcoming Saturday for lunch. I had a party in Boston to go to that Saturday night, so lunch was very convenient. I would make it back to Framingham in plenty of time. Driving up to Leominster took about an hour. I was not too thrilled about the amount of time it took to get there, although in my first long term relationship I would drive four hours to hook up with Jeannie in Montpelier Vermont. That put a real bad taste in my mouth in regards to long distance romance. The relationship was bad, and the travel just made things worse.

 When I arrived at Lisa's apartment, I was impressed that it looked relatively clean, and she had a nice roommate. I drove her to a local diner, and we had a very nice lunch. We laughed at each other's lame jokes, and all seemed right with the world. After lunch, I drove her back to her apartment where we talked more. We were sitting near each other on the side couch in the living room, so I innocently moved ever so closely to her. She smiled at me nervously. I put my arm around her shoulders and quickly kissed her. We spent the next few hours talking and laughing. It was getting late, and I was now actually getting torn between staying with Lisa or going to the party in Boston that was going to begin around 8. I decided to stay. I knew I had found someone special. I left her place around 11 p.m., and felt good about my decision. The day had flown by. I was going to have a Christmas party at my grandparent's house the next weekend, so I invited her, and she accepted.

 The next weekend I invited about 20 of my friends from UMass and from work over for the party. Lisa arrived a little late because of the snowstorm that had been falling all day. I was not sure how this evening was going to end. She obviously could not drive back in a blizzard, so then the question would be where was she going to sleep? We had only been dating a week, so I did not want her to think I was desperate for her. After the party was over, we were alone together. I asked her where she would like to sleep. We just looked at each other. Soon after that awkward moment, we found each other in my master bed. At first it seemed like this was too good to be true, but in the end it was not satisfying for either one of us. It left me both emotionally and physically wounded, and with not much to say the next morning. I did not believe she was ready for a new relationship, and her body told me so by rebelling against me. Even though we did not start off on the right foot, we felt something between us, and kept our relationship moving forward.

 At that time I was the drummer for a rock band called "ThirdPerson". My brother John was the lead singer and keyboardist for the band. We were working on finishing our first album, and touring at all the local clubs in Boston. Lisa would often accompany me to the clubs helping me set up my drums. I was impressed that she never complained about the long hours in between setting up, playing, taking down, and then driving back to Framingham at 2 a.m. Luckily most of our gigs were on Friday or Saturday nights, so it did not interfere with our jobs.

By May 1988, I had asked her to move in with me. She agreed. Her older brother Danny helped her move out of her apartment. He was a little odd. There was something not quite right about him. Even Lisa had told me he was a little strange, but never let on what "It" was. By now, I had been officially divorced from Mary. She was very upset with me, because she thought we should try to work things out, but I knew that it would never work out between us. It was not just the fact that she had cheated on me, but it was how she treated me after the Florida event. She told me that the reason she had cheated was that she wanted to try someone new. And worse, that "He" had been like a fine piece of steak, and I was chopped beef! There was no way to recover a love that was never there. She called me the night before the court date to say that she was not going to go. I told her she had to. She kept asking me, "Why?" Instead of arguing with her, I used my grandmother's line. "You know what you have to do, now do it!" And I hung up the phone. I even picked her up the next morning to take her to the Worcester court. We stopped at a diner on the way in for breakfast. Mary sat there and cried. I felt nothing more than determination to get this sad saga done before I softened and changed my mind. After the court hearing there was nothing left to do, but sell our condo and divvy up the furniture. Thank goodness it was over. I could now begin my new life with Lisa.

A NEW START ∽

It felt good to have someone living with me again. The move in went smoothly, and there really were no issues to deal with. We were both happy with our decisions. Earlier Lisa told me that she would not move in with me unless my intensions were to marry her. I did not feel she was being pushy, more that we were getting dangerously close to age 30, and we did not want to let life pass us by. I had every intention of asking her to marry me, so while vacationing in my family's Mattapoisett cottage that July I popped the question. She knew it was coming because we had picked out the ring together in Boston a few weeks earlier. Fortunately, she said, "Yes", and all was well with the world.

We decided to get married in January, because it gave her 6 months to prepare, and we were hoping that her younger brother Devon would be discharged from his tour of duty on the *USS Nimitz* by then. My family was very excited about our impending nuptials. My 90-year-old grandfather a few months earlier asked if Lisa would marry me, so I knew this was the right girl for me. As the date of our wedding approached, we learned that Devon's tour would not be ending until May. We thought about postponing our wedding date, but we had booked everything from the caterer to sending out the invitations to 130 people. We decided to keep our plans moving forward.

The night before the wedding, my parents put on the formal dinner for our entire immediate family at a local restaurant. It was fun, but I found it strange that none of Lisa's family would give a toast to us when asked by my father. Her dad was a math professor at Fitchburg State College, so he had plenty of experience speaking in front of people. Her brother Danny was acting strange, so I knew something was up with him. The real concern I had was the weather. It had begun to snow heavily earlier in the day. We made it to the church rehearsal in the afternoon, but the drive over to the dinner was a bit precarious. Most of Lisa's family was going to have to drive up from Pennsylvania right into the middle of the blizzard. We received call after call that all of her aunts, uncles, and cousins were not going to make it up for our celebration. I was very sad for Lisa, because I knew how much her family meant to her.

A strange thing happened on the way home from the dinner. Danny was supposed to go back to my parent's house to spend the night, but instead he insisted on staying with us. I really was not very happy, because I wanted to focus my attention on the most important day of my life. I did not want to have to feel like a baby sitter. But Lisa looked up to her older brother, and allowed him to come back home with us. I tried to not have it affect me and stayed up until midnight getting my clothes ready for the wedding, as well as packing for our honeymoon to the Trapp Family Resort in Stowe Vermont.

The following morning was absolutely beautiful. The sun shone brightly, the snow was deep and perfectly white, and the sky was clear and blue. It was the perfect setting for a wedding. All of my family had made it from all points across the country because they had arrived a few days before the storm. We lost 30 people from Lisa's side, but she was a real trooper and did not let her disappointment show. As she walked down the aisle holding her father's arm, I was all choked up. When we had to repeat our vows, I was never able to complete the full sentence. But we made it through the ceremony and walked out into the brilliant sunlight. The reception was held at The Village Hall across the common from the Unitarian Church, which made it easy for all the guests; instead of having to drive, they only had to walk around the massive snow piles.

The reception went without any problems. I was even able to play a song with my brother John after the meal was over. Our faces hurt from smiling so much. It had been a great day. Now it was time to begin our new lives together, but first we had to gather our bags from our house. Danny was there. He said that he would lock up the house after he left. We had made arrangements with our next door neighbor Molly to check in on the house, as well as feed our two cats. We felt we could leave and not worry about anything. We stopped in on my parents for a quick bite before heading to Vermont. I felt we had stayed there a little too long. I wanted to begin my honeymoon. Lisa did not seem all that enthusiastic about going. It felt a little odd. After two hours, we finally were on the road. We decided to stop at the Holiday Inn in Boxborough Massachusetts to spend the night, because it was close to 8:00, and we were exhausted from everything we had just been through. I was excited to consummate our marriage. Once we got settled into our room, I was ready to make love to my new wife. She was not. She fell asleep. I was wide awake with my anticipation dashed, and the disappointment of not doing what a normal newly married couple was suppose to do on their wedding night. Like Lisa, I fell asleep.

OUR HONEYMOON

We drove to Vermont early the next morning after breakfast. I was still a little peeved from the non-action I received on my wedding night. I felt a void. I assumed that now we were rested we would commence our honeymoon in fine fashion in our luxurious lodge. We arrived in Stowe late morning, and were checking in to the Trapp Family by 11:30. I was looking forward to getting settled in and exploring the facility with her. We walked around after eating lunch, and browsed the gift shop. We brought our cross-country skis with us. I was never much of a cross-country skier, because it lacked the rush feeling I got from downhill skiing. Lisa never took up downhill skiing, so I was happy to join her on the trails surrounding the Trapp Family. The only problem was the fact it was bitterly cold. The temperature was well below zero, and with the wind, the cold was even worse. There were fireplaces in many of the lobbies throughout the lodge, so I was ready to snuggle with her. But Lisa was not really in the snuggling kind of mood. I thought after dinner, we could go back to our room, watch a good movie, and then make our own fun. Once again, all she wanted to do was take a bath, and then go to sleep. At this point I was very confused. How could you go from making love and romance while we were dating, to acting like I barely existed? The four days we spent there was fun for a couple that had been together for 20 years, but the way we were interacting was not the way of a newly married couple.

    My grandmother had sent us a note from Florida. She and my grandfather were unable to make our wedding. Her note was full of advice from a woman who had been married twice. Once to my grandfather Lieutenant Colonel Claire Conzelman who never made it home from Corregidor during World War II, and then to my step-grandfather Deane C. Davis who had been the Governor of Vermont in the late 60's and early 70's. We appreciated her thoughtfulness, but I wondered what she would have written if she knew how Lisa was acting now.

    On our second day at The Trapp Family, we received a phone call from our next door neighbor whom we had asked to feed our cats. She said that she was confused, because Danny was still in our house! She felt very uncomfortable going into the house while he was there. We apologized for the confusion, and explained that we had no idea that he would still be there. We told her that we would call him, and ask him to leave at once. That is exactly what we did. He had been there eating our food and watching videos. I felt almost violated. I barely knew the guy, and already he was taking advantage of us. A few days later we were driving back to Framingham. We never made love, and there seemed to be no romance to be found between us. As I was walking down our walkway from the driveway carrying my bags, I felt that the rug had been pulled out from under me. I was very sad. I could not believe that this was happening again to me. At least with Mary, her cruelty was more in my face. With Lisa, her ambivalence with her emotions snuck up from behind. I never saw it coming.

SECRETS

Eventually she caved to her inner need, and we made love. But now I had this subtle doubt deep down that there was something very wrong going on between us. I felt there was a secret hidden within Lisa, and I had the right to know about it. I was now her husband, and there should be no secrets between us. I thought if she just opened up to me, it would make our relationship that much stronger and intimate. But whenever I approached the subject, she made it clear that there was nothing wrong by basically saying, "Back off".

That summer we had fun visiting friends, and vacationing in Mattapoisett and at my grandfather's Morgan Horse farm in Montpelier, Vermont. Lisa's brother Devon was honorably discharged from the Navy, and had arrived home in early May. It was nice getting to know him. He seemed a little aloof and seemed like a real thinker. He loved his sports cars, motorcycles, and top of the line stereo equipment, and because he was single, and in the military for 8 years, he had lots of cash and many toys. He moved back in with his parents in Ashby, Massachusetts to settle back into a non-commissioned life and to find what he was going to do with the rest of his life. He spent much of his time working on his bright orange Datsun 280Z that was parked in the large barn on his dad's property. He could do everything from change a tire to rebuild an engine. He was also good at wielding a hammer. We had him do some odd repair jobs on my grandfather's house. Whenever I tried to help, he would politely say that he was fine and did not need the help. He told his sister that I was a "putz" with a hammer. I was better at writing a check to pay for his help rather than getting in his way.

As the summer was coming to an end, Lisa and I noticed a slight change in Devon's behavior. When he arrived home, he had seemed at peace and very confident. But just a few months later, he began to show signs of depression. We were concerned and asked him what was wrong. He said there was nothing wrong. Lisa asked him to move in with us for a while to help figure things out in his life. I suggested that he look into selling life insurance. But he declined both offers.

By October, he was very down, and could barely look us in the eye any more. His father tried to find out what was going on, and even scolded him to try snapping him out of his funk. Nothing worked. One day when he was in the barn with his father looking over his sports car, he made the odd statement about the jack holding up the car. He said, "If that jack ever slipped and I was under the front wheel, wouldn't that be a bad way to die?" But his dad never said anything about this conversation to any of us.

My brother Will who had moved to Houston Texas invited us for Thanksgiving. We accepted, but Lisa was a little concerned for her brother's welfare. Her parents also were leaving to visit their family in Pennsylvania. The two brothers decided they were going to stay home for the holiday. When the Wednesday before Thanksgiving came, we were packing for our trip in our bedroom. Lisa paused for a moment and said, "I really don't want to go, because I feel there is going to be a death in my family". I did not know what to say, except we have to go, and that everything was going to be ok.

THANKSGIVING DRINKING

When we flew into the Houston airport I was struck by how hot and humid the air was even in late November. I had no desire to ever move into an area like this. When my brother picked us up, I was again struck by how large an area Houston encompassed. It took almost an hour to reach the suburbs of Houston. I noticed all the religious billboards that came one after another, which I was not used to back in the northeast corner of the United States.

It was nice seeing my brother and his wife Ellen and their two-year-old-son Bob. I really enjoyed playing with him. Lisa seemed fine there. She did not bring up her worry about her brother, so that was a relief. We were able to relax. My brother and I played tennis. I had not played in such heat and humidity before. The only positive was that I beat him somehow. When I arrived home, Lisa had put the two single beds together in our room, so that we could make love. I was pleasantly surprised. That night she said that she wanted to go out to the package store to buy some liquor. I thought that this was a little weird, because I had never seen her drink except for the occasional wine at dinner when we went out. But it was a chance to drive around Houston and see the sights. She bought a liter of Jack Daniels. I was wondering why she bought that particular type of booze, and not something else. It seemed like that was awfully strong stuff. I thought the proper thing to do was bring home some wine so that everyone could enjoy it. My family was not that into drinking, and neither was I, so we brought home only the Jack Daniels. I had no interest in drinking anything so strong that would give me a headache. I had learned my lesson back in college.

The next day I noticed the bottle of JD on top of the kitchen counter by the sink. It had been partially consumed. Again, I did not think much about it. My brother Will thought otherwise. Later that day, he came up to me and said, "I am really concerned. Have you noticed the Jack Daniels bottle, and how much is gone?" I said that I was unaware of any problem. He then said, "You have a big problem on your hands, and you had better do something about it." I told him I would bring it up to her. He said, "If you do, I will probably get in trouble for bringing it to your attention." I said not to worry, and that I would be discreet in how I approached the subject.

I did try to ask her why she had drunk so much of the bottle. She said that she was worried about what was going on at home and that it helped to calm her nerves. There was no arguing with that logic, but now it did not sit well with how she was perceived by my brother. Sunday finally came, and it was time to go. Will had not brought up his concern again. He had made his feelings known and knew it was in my hands as to how I was going to handle this very delicate situation.

DEVON'S DEATH

We were happy to be heading home. We were tired, and just wanted to get back to our normal routine. We had to go to work the following day, so I needed to get my head back in the game. My parents said they would be happy to pick us up at the Logan Express terminal in Framingham. When we arrived and got off the bus, they greeted us. They seemed fine and made small talk on the short drive home. But as I was taking our bags from the car trunk, my father took me aside and said there was trouble at Lisa's parents' home. They were not sure what was going on, but they thought Devon was dead. I was totally confused. My father said that Danny had called my sister-in-law Lynne and said that he found Devon in the barn crushed under the driver's side wheel of his sports car. The way he was talking was gibberish and frantic, so it was difficult to understand just what happened.

I turned to Lisa and said that something terrible had happened to Devon and that we needed to get up to Ashby fast. She became very upset and ran into the house to put down her bags and gather some things to bring with her. I walked over to Alex and Molly's house next door to let them know we had arrived home but that something bad had happened to her brother. Molly gave me a hug and told me she loved us. A few minutes later we were back on the road heading to Ashby. Lisa and I did not say much on the way up. When we drove into Fitchburg, she told me to pull into the package store. I figured she needed something to help calm her down. I did not want anything to drink, because I knew I would have to have a level head to deal with what I was about to see.

We arrived on her parent's property by four in the afternoon and were met by her brother Danny. He said that he had tried to call Devon on Thanksgiving Day to find out what he was doing, but there was no answer. He kept trying but figured that he was out with some friends. He tried the following day and that is when he began to get concerned. Danny did not go over to the house until Sunday morning. He went into the house to see if he was in there, but he was not. He looked up at the barn, and saw that the big door was slightly ajar, so he went over to investigate. That is when he saw his brother lying underneath the car. He went over to see if his brother was alive, but he could tell that his brother was dead by the way the front wheel had crushed his chest. In a panic, Danny tried to call the police, but the phone was not working. He kept trying, and finally got through. By the time we arrived, Devon had already been put in a body bag, and driven to the local morgue. The police had questioned Danny as to his reason for being at the house with his brother. I believe they wanted to investigate whether this had been an accident, a suicide, or a murder.

The police had already left the premises, and now we had to stay there in our own confusion waiting for the dreadful moment when the parents would come home to learn of their son's death. I was antsy, so I went into the barn to see for myself the scene of the accident. The car had been jacked back up, but the jack was on the front side bumper of the car. If this had been a suicide, then it would have been very difficult for Devon to reach over, and turn the handle to drop the car on himself. I was told that Danny was jealous of his younger brother, but I could not fathom him going to this much trouble to kill his brother, and then act so distraught. And Devon was an excellent mechanic who would not take chances like this. The jack appeared to be in good working order, because the car was still off the ground from being jacked back up into place. Nothing made sense.

When I left the barn after 20 minutes, I saw the parents' car was in the driveway. They were home. I walked into the house to see Leslie sitting on the couch clutching her handkerchief, crying. Dan senior was in the kitchen with Danny and Lisa in shock at what he had come home to. He said to Danny, "It must have been terrible for you to come across your brother's body." He also told us that he and Leslie had gotten into a fight on the way down to Pennsylvania, and he had almost turned the car around and came home. As Danny and Lisa were walking out of the house, Danny said, "I wish it had been me who died and not Devon." Lisa agreed saying she wished the same for herself. I thought that was a strange thing to say, but I was not going to say anything at that moment. We finally left their house by nine o'clock and arrived home by 10. We were both fried, and ready to go to bed. It was going to be a difficult week with trying to work, and at the same time prepare for a funeral that never should have happened.

DEVON'S FUNERAL

Lisa was very upset. Her mind was not on work, and was given most of the week off from her job at Symco Labs. She found herself missing exits while driving home from work, so it was better to focus on the preparations for Devon's funeral. I accompanied her every day back and forth to her parent's home. It was a very numb time. I got to meet all the relatives who could not make our wedding for the first time at the funeral. Going through Devon's small bedroom was strange, because everything was just as it was suppose to be as of the day he died. Lisa was angry at her mother for washing his clothes. She wanted to smell the scent of her brother one last time. I did not say much. There was nothing I could say that would ease the family's pain. I felt a bit as an outsider, because I really never got to know Devon. I saw him only a smattering of times, so I had no real connection to his life.

One night during the week, Danny was in the kitchen speaking angrily, and slurring his words. His father said, "We are going to celebrate Devon's life. Why can't you?" It was a very awkward moment, and it made me feel very uncomfortable. Danny kept saying that he was going to "lose it". I hoped not. It was a very tense time anyway. I did not want to have to deal with any more than was placed on our plate.

The morning before the funeral, the immediate family was to have a private viewing of Devon lying in the casket. I was not looking forward to this time, because I felt it was going to be over the top in emotion. Lisa and I walked into the room where Devon lay, and we both began to cry. Lisa was accompanied by her mom and they both stared down and stroked his face. His upper body was exposed, and the rest was covered by the casket. He looked pale, but pretty much the same as he did in life. Then Danny appeared around the back entrance of the funeral home. He just stopped and stared for a moment, and then he walked up to see his brother for the last time. He was shaken, and again I wondered if he was really going to lose it during the service. The funeral director asked Dan if during the wake the family would like the casket open for viewing. Dan implicitly replied, "Absolutely not". The director asked again, "Are you sure, because many of his family members and friends would like to see him one last time." Dan made it perfectly clear that he did not want an open casket. I thought this did not make any sense. Devon looked fine, and it would be healing for the rest of the family to say good-bye. But the casket was closed, and it was the last time we would ever see Devon again. After the funeral his body was cremated, and his ashes were kept at the family home.

OVERWHELMING ~

After the funeral, we all stood in the receiving line to greet the friends and extended members of Lisa's family. Devon had many friends, and it was nice to meet them. I wished that I had been able to get to know him better. It was a very brief encounter that I had with him, so I never got to know what made him tick. I did know that he was a very private and gifted individual. His only downfall was that he came home to his very dysfunctional family and apparently did not know how to deal with a family that was so flawed. He never said anything to any of us, but I am assuming that he was very disappointed, so much so that he could not live with his mental anguish.

I will always wonder what really happened the day that he died. Was he so depressed that he actually took his own life? He even had told his dad that it would be an interesting way to die if his car fell on top of him. The other possibility was that when Danny came to visit, he found that Devon was prone underneath his car and out of jealousy and anger turned the handle on the jack and killed his younger brother because the week before they had gotten into a big fight where Devon had flattened him to the ground, after a bitter exchange. There were no witnesses, so the only one we could ask was Danny, and he was in no shape to answer questions.

I finally understood why he acted so strangely, because he had a real issue with alcohol. He was a verbally abusive alcoholic. I had not seen this side of him before, because I did not have much interaction with him, but since our wedding I had more than my share of time spent in his presence. He made me feel very uncomfortable. I often dreaded having to be around him, but the family was trying to figure out what they should do about him. Don, Sr. would often say to him, "Why don't you just find a job?" The problem was that he was often inebriated, and would soon not show up, or if he did, it would be quite apparent that he was in no condition to work. I had not realized how big an issue his sickness was until I spent time going back and forth to their home in Ashby. I was thinking how blessed Lisa was that she did not have this same problem that Danny was exhibiting. Hers was more driven by her circumstances, rather than as an alcoholic. I was hoping that she and I could keep our distance away from her brother, so that we would not have to deal with his crazy behavior. I was not very good at confrontation, especially not with an irrational person. Nothing I could say would do any good anyway.

I had to walk a fine line of not saying too much, and insulting her brother, and at the same time protecting my home from insanity. Lisa had been dealing with this for a long time, so she appeared to have a handle on her brother. My main focus was to make sure Lisa was going to be all right, and that I could support her through her time of grieving.

My job kept me busy, and my rock band ThirdPerson had recently released our first album. In fact, my brother John brought the albums in the back of his car to Devon's funeral. We had been playing out in the Boston local club scene for the past three years, and this album was the culmination of many years of hard work. I was thrilled that these songs were being played on the local radio stations such as WBCN and WAAF. My focus was moving our band forward in the hopes that we might have the opportunity to be signed by a national label. I thought that Lisa might too get caught up in the hype of our band, which would take some of her mind off this terrible time in her life. She was working a new full time job at Symco Labs, and that too I felt would be good for her. Her friends there would also give her the support that she needed. So we tried to move on the best that we knew how. My mother came over one night to check in on how Lisa was holding up. The three of us sat in our living room and cried for quite a while. My mother talked about losing her dad during World War II while he was stationed on Corregidor. He had been captured by the Japanese, while he tried to hold onto "The Rock" of the Philippines with his undermanned army. He never made it home alive. Lisa's sadness brought out my mother's, and we had a good cry. It was nice that my mother could bare her soul. I hoped that would help heal both of their broken hearts.

CONFUSED ON NANTUCKET

My parents had invited the entire immediate family to have a reunion on Nantucket Island to help celebrate their wedding anniversary the weekend after the fourth of July. I was excited that I would be seeing my brothers and their wives and my nephews. I always enjoyed swimming into the large waves and body surfing. I told Lisa about it thinking this would be a nice break, but she was not thrilled about going. She said that she just started her new position at Symco Labs and could not possibly go. I said that it was only for the weekend, and we did not have to leave until she was done work. She insisted that she would probably have to work on the weekend too. I was confused. I knew that she could at least ask her new boss. Surely he would understand that this was an important family function, and that she could always make up the time. Plus, it was summer time. Many of her peers were taking time off, so I could not understand why she would not even give it a shot.

In the end, I took the ferry with my entire family, but without her. We had a fun, but stressful time. Both my brothers had young children. John and Lynne had their new baby boy Sid with them. As new parents it was not easy attending a family function, and tending to a new baby. My other nephew Bob was three and going through the latter part of the "Terrible Twos", but overall he was pretty well behaved. The family group picture was taken in front of the inn where we were staying. It was a nice picture, except one important person was missing. I felt empty without her. I liked showing off my new wife, and with her not being there it sent a weird message to the rest of the family. Something felt really wrong and out of place. The weekend came to an end, and we all took the 3:00 ferry back to Hyannis.

When I arrived home, Lisa was there. She was not really interested in hearing about the trip, and I did not feel like talking about it. She told me that she had spoken to her best friend Robin who lived in California with her new husband and that she was coming to visit us that next weekend. I was happy that Lisa was excited to see her friend whom she had not seen in quite some time. Lisa had been in amateur theater productions with Robin, and their most memorable play was the Wizard of Oz where Lisa played Dorothy. Lisa had taken a few years off from college to find herself, and the theater had given her direction and added structure to her life. But she knew that this would be a short lived experience, because she needed to finish her degree at Fitchburg State College and find a career that suited her talents.

Robin arrived, and I was happy to see her. She always had a smile on her face, and she seemed grounded. I felt calm around her. I knew that she would help Lisa through her grieving process. One day we were all sitting in the living room together.

"I need a hug", I said jokingly to Lisa.
Lisa said, "No".
"Please!" I replied half heartedly,
Again she said, "No".
Robin chimed in, "Just give him a hug!"
"I just can't!" Lisa exclaimed.

So that made me feel sad, and Robin looked bewildered. Soon after, we got on the conversation of sex, and who they had "done" in their theater group. Both had sex with their producer and Lisa had a yearlong affair with Bill who had played the Cowardly Lion. I asked if they had ever done a ménage a trois. They both said no, but Robin said that she would like to try.

"Really?" I said.

"Absolutely!" she said.

I knew she was serious, and I even thought seriously about entertaining the idea of having great sex with her and my wife. But that fantasy was quickly quelled when Lisa made it clear that she was not interested. That was the closest I ever came to living out every man's dream.

A STRANGE LETTER

A few weeks later, I came home from work to find Lisa not in the house, so I walked into the dining room to find an open letter on the table. It was out in the open, so I decided to read it. It was a letter to her best friend Robin. As I read it, I was taken aback about who I reading about. It was not about me but about some guy she had met at work. She went into detail about the common interests they shared with cats and that he was a very nice person. My mind once again went numb. Could this be happening to me again? She knew about Mary, so why was she almost advertising the fact that she was either having an affair or going to have one? This was very bizarre behavior. Then I thought, maybe she is trying to stop herself from making a very big relationship-changing mistake. Since she was not home, I had time to get my thoughts and emotions together. I did not know into what direction this now found information was going to take us, but I knew I had to figure out how I was going to approach her—delicately or otherwise.

There was no turning back, so I decided to go for a walk around the neighborhood just to clear my head before she came home. I left the letter where I had found it and then started walking. I kept saying to myself, "I can't believe this is happening to me again!" I was also pissed, because I felt I had given her plenty of support after her terrible loss with her brother. Now I had to once again confront a cheater, and that is the last thing I wanted to do. Marriage was all about trust and support, and all of a sudden I had neither.

After 20 minutes I walked back towards my grandparent's home, and saw in the distance her Toyota parked in our small driveway. I was just tired enough that I did not come in too excited. Lisa was in the kitchen, so I walked up to her emotionless and said, "We have to talk". She followed me into the dining room, and I pointed at the letter. I asked, "What is this about?" She looked at the letter, and said that he was just a friend and that she only wanted to have coffee with him. I asked who he was, and she replied, "It doesn't matter". She also said that he meant nothing to her. I said, "Then why did you write about him to your best friend?" She said that there was nothing to worry about and that nothing happened.

I tried to believe her, but there was nagging doubt. I said it might be a good time to make an appointment with our psychologist Meghan to discuss this, and find out what in the world was really going on. The next day I called Meghan and told her about the letter, and that I needed to get to the bottom of what was really happening. We were back in her office a few days later. We focused on Lisa being so elusive to me, and what was going on with this new guy. Lisa said that I was not home during the week very much, and that she was lonely. All she wanted to do was have coffee with him. I finally could not contain myself anymore, and I blurted out, "Have you gone to bed with him?" Lisa just looked at me calmly, and said no, but not convincingly enough to put away my doubt.

Meghan seemed satisfied with our session, and thought everything would be fine between us. In my mind nothing had been resolved, and now there was this aching feeling in the back of my mind that would always be there. I spoke to Robin a few days later on the phone about the letter. She said, "Oh yea, the guy at work". I tried to get a little more information, but she was too much a friend to Lisa, and would not give me anymore details. Lisa did not seem at all put out with my finding her letter, the session with Meghan, or my conversation with Robin. I never liked secrets, and with each passing day there seemed to be more of them piling up not only from her past, but now her present too.

MORE FAMILY SECRETS ~

I could not believe how fast 1988 had whipped by. First our marriage at the beginning of the year in January, followed by Devon's death in November on Thanksgiving Day. Both events were landmark moments in our lives. One day we were joyously happy and at the next event, full of sadness. We decided to spend Christmas Day dinner with her parents and Danny, figuring that they would need our support. My parents were heading off to Texas to be with Will and his family, so it all worked out for us to spend time with Lisa's family. Their house was very quaint and full of rustic country charm. Her dad was a semi-retired math professor at Fitchburg State College, and her mother was working at a local factory as an administrative assistant. As far as I could tell, they were very nice down-to-earth, friendly people. The only clue that I could see was that Devon had been very depressed after coming home from his tour on the *USS Nimitz*. I thought that was normal for a person who knew exactly what each day was going to entail for most of his young working life, only now to be cast adrift into the real world without having any direction of what to do next. Danny was odd, and I knew there was something going on with him, but no one had straight out told me that he had a problem with alcohol.

I enjoyed the smell of the turkey cooking in the oven, as well as helping to set up the table for the big dinner. For a little while it was Lisa, myself, and her parents chatting away and enjoying each other's company, and then Danny arrived. He was acting strange, and you could feel the atmosphere in the room change from happy to tense. After an hour, it was time to sit down for dinner. I was starving and could not wait to dig in. I was sitting next to Lisa's mom Leslie, when for a moment everyone had gone back into the kitchen to get more food. It was just me and her mom sitting at the table. She turned to me and said, "You know, Danny told me that Dan had molested Lisa. What do you think of that?" The next second, everyone was back from the kitchen sitting at the table. My mind was racing with confusion. I did not know what to say or what to do. A few minutes later, Leslie said to Dan, "So how is it with that woman that you're having fun with?" He replied, "What, you think that I am having an affair?" Nothing more was said. I just looked at Lisa, and she looked at me. I felt very awkward, and now was looking forward to leaving as soon as possible. But they had made plans to see some of Devon's old friends after dinner, so we decided to go with them. Both Leslie and Dan acted like everything was fine, but now I knew differently. I needed time to talk with Lisa about a very sensitive subject, and I did not know when the right time would be, but I knew I had to do it soon.

AGONIZING QUESTIONS ~

A few days went by, as I agonized over how I was going to approach this very delicate subject of molestation. I kept thinking, "What if I was wrong?" But why would her mother make such a damaging accusation against her own husband? Finally I got the nerve up to ask Lisa. She was sitting at the dining room table about to have lunch, when I just blurted it out.

"Were you molested by your father?"

"Why?" she asked. "Who told you that?"

"Your mother," I said, "while we were having lunch."

I was dumbfounded! I did not know what to say next. I gave her a big hug and said that we should probably have a session with our psychologist Meghan. She agreed. I did not want to know more, because I was already confused and dealing with emotional overload. I also thought that Meghan would know how to discuss this new-found information better than I could.

I made the appointment right away, and we were in her Acton office a few days later. Lisa sat next to Meghan, and I sat across from them looking at both of them waiting for someone to speak.

Meghan took a deep breath, and said, "Well, what would you like to ask Lisa?"

"I don't understand," said. "How could this happen to you? "And why didn't you tell me sooner?"

Lisa said that she had already told Meghan about her being molested and that they were just waiting for the right time to tell me. They did not think that anyone else would say anything to me, especially her mother! Lisa told me that from the time she had been a baby to when she finally moved out at 17 that her father had been molesting her. I could not believe it! No one did anything to protect her, not even her own mother! I was pissed. Now I knew, as the Weyman family onion began to be peeled back, that more and more crazy information was being revealed.

I was not sure what I was going to do next, or how I was to react. Now that I knew that her father had committed a monstrous act over the span of many years, I thought I needed to do something. Devon was dead and Danny was drinking himself into oblivion. There was definitely a connection to this whole, weird family dynamic. It was very clear that Dan Senior had molested at least one of his children, and his wife had turned a blind eye to his actions. If the brothers had known what was happening, I am sure they needed an advocate in their mother to protect them. But again, she had done nothing, so their father had easy access to them whenever he needed a "quickie". Meghan tried to explain as best she could by showing me a picture of Lisa as a little girl, and saying, "Why not? She is beautiful and innocent. Why not?"

I felt sickened. I could not fathom how anyone could hurt his own child. But he did. And now I knew too much. I felt handcuffed, because I wanted to drive up to the Ashby Police station, and turn this son of a bitch in, but without Lisa backing me up, it was my word against the crime. So, I let Lisa decide how she wanted to handle her father going forward. There was nothing for me to do, but be patient and wait for her next move.

LISA'S COURAGE ~

During the next few months, Meghan suggested to Lisa to tie her family off. In other words, to shut them all out completely. The family sickness had to be quelled for the time being while she tried to get her life back together. I was all for it, but I knew that her parents and brother relied on Lisa's steady hand to guide them. Without her they would act even more dysfunctional and lost. But I told her that I would back her 100%, and not let them in no matter how much they begged. It did not take long for Leslie to begin calling and asking what was going on. I felt slightly guilty about closing the door in her face, but there was no other way to keep the pain away from Lisa.

After a month, Lisa spoke to Meghan at one of their private sessions, and they thought a one-on-one session with her mother might help in the healing process for both of them. Lisa contacted her mother and asked her to join with her and Meghan. Leslie agreed. I would have liked to have been there, but it was not a place for me. Pure and simple it was going to be a session about why Leslie did not protect her defenseless daughter.

The meeting took place, and Lisa reported back to me very little about their discussion. But what she did say was that she did ask her mother why she did nothing to protect her. Apparently her mother broke down and as she was crying, said that she had done the best she could bringing up three children. I was not impressed. There was no admission to her actions, and no apology for ruining her children's lives. I lost any respect that I had for her. At this time, I did not want any further contact with her.

Leslie complained to Lisa that after she had been shut out, she had no one to grieve with. All she had was a drunken son who gave her nothing but grief and a husband who was cruel and emotionless to her.

I gave Lisa a lot of credit for speaking to her mother. She did not receive the apology that she was looking for or any closure to years of torment. Lisa realized that her relationship with her mother was now on life support and knew that she needed more time to figure out in what direction she wanted them to go.

While Lisa's courage was up, Meghan made one more very important request, and that was to have the same conversation with her father. Lisa did not hesitate to agree. She called Dan, and made an appointment for the three of them. I was amazed that Lisa had the courage to confront this perpetrator. I was most worried that she would once again be disappointed and that this would hinder her recovery. But the fact that she was going to ask him why he would have hurt her for so many years was going to be cathartic. I had no idea what was going to happen at this meeting. I could not fathom how he was going to respond, especially talking about his actions in front of a stranger.

The meeting went as planned. I was anxiously waiting at home for her to arrive so I could ask her what happened. When she came home, she looked fine, so I gave her a few minutes before asking her the million dollar question. When we did sit down to speak, she did not give me all that much information, except that Mary was disappointed that she did not grill Dan more. Meghan felt that she had let him off the hook. They both danced around the molestation topic. I believe that Meghan found that she was in over her head dealing with such a man and that he had manipulated his way out of admitting that he had done anything wrong. To me this was unacceptable, especially since this was the one chance that Lisa had to find out the reason why he had done terrible things to her as a little girl. Somehow he got away with it again, and once again, no one did a thing to stop him. Even though I was let down, I was very proud of Lisa for her courage.

KEEPING THEM TIED ~

It was not easy keeping her parents, and brother at bay, because they would call to try and wiggle their way back into our lives. Lisa held firm, and when I answered the phone, I kept it very short. We both would say that Meghan had told us that we needed time to ourselves to regroup as our own family and not be brought back into the family crisis. In other words, "Back off". We needed to heal. It would be months before we allowed any of them to visit. We did go to a few family functions where they attended, but we made sure we mingled with the rest of her aunts, uncles, and cousins, so that we did not find ourselves back trapped in their muck.

One day I did speak to her mother Leslie, and she complained that she had no one to speak to or grieve with. I felt it was just more manipulation, and I wanted us to pull even further away and hopefully not see them again. But of course, that was not going to be realistic. Lisa was pulled back to her family because that is all she ever had known. So finally we acquiesced, and allowed her mother to come down to Framingham to visit us. I was not thrilled to see her. I had lost a lot of respect for her. I could not imagine a mother not protecting her own daughter, and then denying that she had any responsibility or even knowing that it had occurred. My relationship with her had changed forever, and I was not about to trust her again.

MOVING ON ~

For most of the spring and summer, we worked on my grandparent's house. The deal with the family was that we could live there rent free until Nan and Pop passed away, then the house would either be sold to us or sold to the public. Any work we paid for, including sweat equity would reduce our overall payment. We painted all the rooms, had new cedar siding put up and, as well, replaced all the old windows on the second floor. I liked the idea of buying the family homestead where my father and uncles grew up. There was a lot of history there. The only negative was that it had the depressing look of house built around the time of the Great Depression, but with a lot of strokes, we changed the feel of the interior of the house.

Both of my grandparents were living at the Kathleen Daniels Nursing Home just a few miles away. Pop died first, and then my grandmother, imprisoned by her Alzheimer's disease, died a few years later. Now that they were gone, we had to make a fairly quick decision, because my brothers, and my cousins would need the money from the sale of the house to purchase their own homes.

Lisa and I had been looking at homes in the surrounding towns for the past year. We found one in Holliston that had over two acres of land and a gutted metal trailer if we wanted to someday have horses. It abutted the local lake, so it made our decision to put an offer down rather easy. We discovered a problem during the inspection. There was a small open stream going through the den of the house! We could smell the musty air coming from behind the closed cabinet door that was hiding this problem. The Realtor could see the disappointment in our faces and tried to put a positive spin on this new revelation. But in the end, we decided not to go forward with the purchase. My parents had come with us, and they were not thrilled with the house. The Realtor made a snide remark, saying, "I knew the deal was dead when I heard your parent's negative comments".

I was very glad that we did not buy the house from him, because he never had our best interest in mind. It was at that point that one night while walking around the family homestead, I turned to Lisa and said that we should go ahead and buy the house. My father had reported to us that the price on the house, after deducting all the work we had paid and put into it was a mere $107,000! It was a no brainer, because there would already be a ton of equity if we needed to take out an equity line of credit or sell and upgrade one day.

Our decision was made, until the next day when one of Lisa's friends at the animal shelter where she had volunteered told her about a foreclosed house that was for sale on the other side of Route 9. This woman, who was a Realtor, said that the house was going for far less than its value, and that it would be perfect for us. The next day we drove the mile to the house located just a block away from Framingham Centre. It had five bedrooms, two and half baths and was sitting on almost a one acre lot. It had a large country kitchen and a deck. Everything was already there, and we would not have to remodel the other house. We were very excited to learn that the price was only $169,900. We made plans to look at the house with my parents and my brother John, as well as my cousins who were visiting for the Christmas holiday. They all loved the place. The one room that sold me was the den that had been built around the time of Paul Revere.

A few days after Christmas, we were in the Realtor's office signing the paperwork to begin the process of buying the house. We felt very lucky to be first in line to buy such a house. Now all there was to do was have the inspection completed. A few weeks later we met with the inspector and the Realtor. There was still plenty of snow on the ground and on the roof, so it was difficult to see what shape the shingles were in. As the inspector walked around the house, he said, "This is such a big house, that it will nickel and dime you to death". But he found nothing inherently wrong with the overall structure, so we decided to move forward. Of course looking back, the house did not nickel and dime us—it cost us additional thousands to replace the roof and to continually repaint the old cedar shingles that would soon need to be completely replaced.

The excitement of buying this new old house helped to divert our attention to the underlying problem of our relationship but for now we were both on the same page.

MOVING IN ～

We closed on our 198 Maynard Road house in March of 1991. There was still plenty of snow on the ground, which made it difficult to navigate all the large pieces of furniture that were to be transported just 2 miles from where we had lived for the past three years. It was going to be fun working on our own house, which would give us a new start, and something positive to focus on. The land was different. Instead of a very large hill that was virtually useless, but had a gorgeous view, we now had a smaller hill that we could use for sledding. There was also plenty of room to start a garden, and Lisa had always enjoyed getting her hands dirty.

As the snow began to melt off the roof and land, we noticed that the roof was not in as good shape as we had hoped. It would need to be replaced. There was also a concrete cylinder in the upper part of the yard that seemed odd. My father-in-law said that it was probably an old well and that I could start to fill it with dirt and rocks. As I rolled a large rock into it, I felt that something did not feel right. With a little research, I discovered that the town sewer did not connect to our house as it had said in the specs of the Realtor's report. We had the original cesspool that had been built along with the house in 1922. All the other houses on our street were on town sewer. We were just low enough and not lucky enough to be able to tie in. The Baptist pastor in the little church across the street was only tied in because he had a pump to transport the waste 200 feet to the top of the street.

After speaking to our Realtor Carol, she said that their firm would pay for repairing any wear and tear on our cesspool. I thought that was fair, but I still did not like the idea of not being tied into the town. There was also a new law that had recently passed called Title 5 stating that if your cesspool or septic system failed the inspection at the time of house sale, then a new septic system would have to be installed at the owner's expense! I tried not to worry about it, because I was not planning on moving again for a very long time.

The 19 Church Street house that we had lived in was put on the market after painting the walls and doing the final repairs that would make the house sell quickly. The rest of the family was given first right of refusal of the house. No other family showed any interest, so the day the For Sale sign went out in front of the white picket fence we had built, a young couple walked up and asked if they could look around. A day later, our Realtor Carol made another sale. The era of the Greeley family homestead in Framingham was now over. When it came time to sign the paperwork to release their interest in the house, my father and my two uncles looked very sad. Lisa and I needed our independence from the rest of the family, so this seemed like a very positive step.

Within the first full month of moving into our new home, Lisa came home from work one day after stopping at the local pharmacy, and told me that she was pregnant. She had been off the pill for a little while, but we had no idea how quickly and easily she would get pregnant. So here we were with a new house, and now a baby on the way that was due the end of December. The kitchen was in bad shape. It was a 70's style kitchen, but many of the cabinets were in disrepair, so we decided to use some of the gift money that my grandmother Nannie Deane had given us to redo the kitchen and the upstairs bathroom. Our Realtor referred us to her brother who was a carpenter. When we met Bob, he seemed trustworthy. His prices were not too high and were within our budget. After finishing the kitchen for under $10,000, we had him redo the porch off the living room and make a portion of the unfinished basement into a playroom. I had the dual job of fixing up the yard by cutting dead trees, and repairing the grass, as well as painting the baby's room. Lisa worked on putting everything in its place from the move. There were still many unopened boxes to unpack.

    Lisa was still working full time, but by October her feet were really bothering her, and she went on medical leave. I was very happy that she could rest and focus on the baby. I was very excited that the baby was going to be born around the holidays with all of our family being around to celebrate the birth of another baby. It was during the summer that my brother John and his wife Lynne approached us to ask if it would be ok to look at the house right next door. Soon after we had moved in, the house on the corner of Maynard and Pleasant Street went on the market due to a divorce settlement. We had no problem with them buying the house. They had their three-year-old son Sid and their second child was on the way due the following April. I envisioned having a blast with John playing music and sports, having the wives support and baby sit for one another, and the cousins having fun together.

    They closed on the house in September, and began to move in. The first day that I saw them in the house, we just waved to each other. I had this uneasy feeling in my gut that this might not be the perfect set-up that I had originally envisioned. But with the holidays approaching fast there was not time to worry. The holidays were fun, but the anticipation of our new baby arriving kept being pushed off. Our doctor said that there was no sign that the baby was going to come on its own, so he thought it was best to schedule a C-section right after the New Year on January 2nd. I thought that was a bit strange. Why could we not have him perform the surgery before the end of the year? The baby was going to be almost two weeks late, and I was thinking about getting the tax deduction for my new dependent. The doctor said that he would be up in Maine with his family during the holidays, so we would have to wait unless the baby had other ideas. The baby did not, so we enjoyed Christmas and watched Lisa get even bigger.

BABY

I was very nervous on New Year's Day 1992. I was hoping that our baby would decide to come out the usual way, so that we could avoid surgery. Many things could go wrong, worst of which Lisa could die. I had to believe our doctor knew what he was doing and that I just had to let go of my fears. Lisa seemed very calm, and did not say much of anything. We had to be at the hospital in the morning by 6 a.m., so we both slept lightly through the night.

Lisa was already packed, so the 10-minute trip was easy. We checked into the MetroWest Hospital, and walked to her room where she was immediately prepped for surgery. By 7 a.m. she was being rolled down to the operating room to begin our new lives. I was allowed to enter the OR after 20 minutes of the operation beginning. I stood by the right side of her head where I was able to see over the sheet that hid the parts that were being performed by the doctor and nurses. I was able to see a portion of her belly that had gone under the knife. I tried not to look too closely, because I thought I might faint. I became woozy only when I saw the skin around the area that had been cut folded back. I had to sit in one of the stools to recover my composure. Lisa had tears streaming down her face, not because of any pain, but more from the intense emotion that she felt.

I heard the baby begin to cry even before they had lifted him out of her. Yes, it was a boy! His name was going to be Andrew meaning "strong and manly", and his middle name was going to be James as in James T. West, the actor in "The Wild Wild West" TV series. I was thrilled. He was over 10 pounds, and he was beautiful. I could see why there was no way he was coming out vaginally. The nurses pulled him out for Lisa and me to see him for the first time, then the doctor cut his umbilical cord, and the nurses transported him to the nursery.

I remained with Lisa for a few more minutes, and then I was asked to leave the OR while they put her organs back into their proper positions in her belly and stitched her back up. I immediately called my parents to let them know they had a new grandson, and then I called Lisa's mother Leslie. She was angry that I had not called her first. How she assumed that I had not was weird.

"So, I am sure you called your parents first!" she said.

This is why I did not want to call her right away.

My parents and brother drove to the hospital to look in on Lisa and the baby. It was surreal to have a son. I now had a huge responsibility to live up to, but I was really excited all at the same time. I was happy that Lisa and I could just chill out while she was recuperating from her surgery, and I could focus on making sure the nursery was all set up for Andrew. I enjoyed the peace of having time to myself, and to the anticipation and excitement of my child coming home to live with us.

Leslie drove down to the hospital with Danny, who

appeared angry and drunk. I was pissed that she would bring him knowing that he would be in this state. I did not want him in the room with Lisa acting like an asshole, so I brought him to the cafeteria to get something to eat that might help him sober up. I really did not want this responsibility, and I felt abused that I had to put up with Leslie's problem. I think she thought it would be good for him to meet his nephew, but at the same time not being realistic in the fact that he would be upset that his sister was getting the attention and that the spotlight was not on him. He would also have to look at his life, and know that he was a failure. So my job at this point was to get him sober and to lessen the possibility that he might lash out at any of us. I was very glad that they were only going to stay for an hour. I could then focus on the two loves of my life.

HOME WITH BABY

Lisa stayed in the hospital for four days recovering from her operation. I made a bed for her in our living room so that she would not have to climb the stairs up to the second floor. I also had a crib for Andrew in the same room to make it easier for her to take him out to feed him during the day and part of the night. I was very glad to have my family back in our home. I enjoyed the time alone for a few days getting the house in order and going back and forth to the hospital, but now it was time to begin our new life as a family.

At the same time that the baby was coming home, I had volunteered to help coach youth hockey for a team made up of 12-year-olds. I had also been giving drum lessons at our local music store to three students. The money was good, and it kept my chops up for the time that I had not been playing with a band. I soon realized that having a baby took up a lot of my time, and I felt guilty leaving Lisa home alone to tend with the baby on and off on weekends. I finally gave up the hockey coaching, and by the summer I quit giving lessons at the Centre Music House.

    I found that I was very good in working and teaching kids. I think part of the reason I thought it was a good idea to coach and teach was to help get me acclimated on how to interact with children. I had no idea what kind of father I was going to be. My father had been a terrific coach and playmate, but he was not that interested in helping around the house with chores. In fact, I do not remember even being asked to do the dishes. I did mow the lawn, but that is something I liked to do.

    My role now was much more hands-on with chores and feeding and changing Andrew. I thought it was the most amazing sight seeing him nursing on Lisa's breast. What a wonderful way to feed a child. Andrew stopped breast-feeding within 9 months, so I got good at feeding him with the bottle and Gerber fruit and spinach. I loved picking him up, and holding him. He was big and beautiful and a blast to hang out with. I took him out in the stroller whenever the weather was good, and every day that I got home from work. I felt it was my duty to give Lisa a break from having to be a mommy all day. For the first year with Andrew in our lives, all felt right. I did not see any signs of Lisa drinking, and her mother liked to stay over and help out with the baby. As long as she was helpful, and not too interfering, I thought it was fine. My job during the week kept me busy, and we had enough money to live on one income.

    My grandmother Nannie Deane was trying to reduce the size of her taxable estate by giving all of her grandchildren and their wives $10,000 each for a Christmas gift. We used the money to not only help to pay bills, but also do some renovations on our house. We had to put on a new roof, as well as blow in insulation and paint the exterior of the house. The shingles were very old, and we soon found out that the paint would not hold for more than a year before it would start to peel.

Our carpenter had referred a painter who seemed to know what he was doing. He also did not know his own boundaries. I saw him put his arms around Lisa's shoulders when he was talking to her right in front of me! She did not pull away, which gave me an uneasy feeling. I found her in the downstairs bathroom with him one day not saying anything, just looking at him. I quickly made it known that I was there. She came out and gave me a guilty kiss. The next time I spoke with our carpenter, I told him that I was not pleased with the way he was making himself available to my wife. Our carpenter George asked him to leave the project, so the problem was resolved. It made me quite aware that my wife had an eye for other men, but I was hoping that she would not act on her feelings. I did not have a whole lot of trust for her, so my guard was up to protect my heart.

We decided to do the job of having the existing shingles removed and replaced with new cedar shingles that would be pre-primed before the new paint went on. It cost a lot more money than we thought, but in the end the paint would hold for another 10 years without any hint of peeling. The new painter whom we hired was older and professional in the way he spoke to us. This time I had no worries about anyone hitting on my wife.

SPIRITUAL GROWTH ~

I had been grappling with my identity, and trying to figure out what I wanted to do with the rest of my life as far as work and my career. I had been working in my life insurance career for over 10 years, and I did not feel as though I was progressing as the rest of my peers had done. I had reached a mental and financial plateau, and I needed something to recharge my enthusiasm for what I was doing. I heard about the Hoffman Quadrinity Process from my parents. They had friends that had attended and found it very helpful in unlocking their lives from their past childhood. In other words, it got them unstuck from their own stinking thinking.

At this point I was ready to try just about anything. I attended the introductory meeting that was held in a home in Southborough Massachusetts. It sounded interesting, and my parents wanted to do something nice for me, so they offered to pay the $2,500 fee. I was very thankful for their offer, and I took them up on it. The 10-day session was going to be held in the middle of November down in Little Compton Rhode Island right near the ocean. I really did not know what I was getting myself into, but I knew it could not hurt my current situation. The day I was going to leave, I played with Andrew who was nearing his second birthday. He was wearing a plastic fireman's helmet and looked really cute. I did not want to leave him or Lisa behind for so much time, but I had committed to the program, so I drove the two hours to the compound where the activities were to be held.

When I first arrived I was feeling quite vulnerable, as I watched the other attendees arrive one by one. We all just quietly stared politely at each other. I could tell that everyone was feeling the same awkwardness that I was feeling, so I did not feel so bad. It felt like this journey I was taking was going to be one that I would not feel alone. I saw one very attractive blond woman who I found interesting and fun to look at. She seemed very innocent and kept to herself. She looked up at me, but then looked away. I did not want to appear too creepy, so I looked away too towards the other participants. Once everyone arrived, the director had us meet in the main conference area to explain what we were going to be doing the first few days. After we met for 20 minutes, and introduced each other, we then were told to meet with our counselors. I had a young man who asked me what I was feeling most guilty about. I told him that I had stolen something from the local boat yard when I was 12, and that it had made me feel horrible about myself. He looked me in the eyes, and said, "Well, your mother let you down."

I was taken aback by what he just said. I was not trying to place the blame on anyone but myself. I was the one that had stolen not my mother. I tried to understand what he was trying to do. The only thing I could make out of this was that my mom had issues and had not handled her own feelings, but had passed them on to me. I really was not going to judge my mother on any past failings she might have done, but I was going to keep going with this process, because I knew something good would come from it.

After dinner the first night there, we were brought back into the main room to be instructed as to what we were going to do for the next four hours. We were each to take a whiffle ball bat, and proceed to strike a pillow while yelling out the name of whatever person was angering us the most. This technique was to help begin the process of getting out in the open what had been stuffed away since our childhood. At first I was a little embarrassed as to what I was yelling. Swearing at my parents for any wrongs that they had done me in front of these strangers was not an easy task, except for the fact that everyone else was doing it at the same time I was. There was a lot of yelling and crying that first night. I did feel a sense of relief. And a lot did come out. Mostly guilt and resentment was, for the first time, given light and was now able to be removed once and for all.

One day the assignment was to write a scathing letter to my father and then my mother. It had to be 30 pages within one hour each! I thought this assignment verged on the impossible, but I did it. After I gave the written work to the instructor, he said, "Nice going. Now write a letter to your parents saying nothing but wonderful things about them. Same thing... 60 pages!"

My right hand felt like it was going to fall off or worse, turn into a claw. But I did it, and I felt a real sense of accomplishment. Fortunately, I did not have to do another lengthy assignment like that one again. The next writing assignment was even more intriguing. We were driven to a cemetery and had to write about what people would be saying about us after we were dead. I wrote about how some people would be laughing, because of the funny things that I have done. Pranks and such, but this was not acceptable. I was driven back to the cemetery with a few of the other attendees who also had not gotten it right. This time I wrote more methodically, and depressingly. Needless to say I got it right this time.

One night, after a long day of beating my pillow, and going through a variety of mental excises, I was very much ready to go to bed and fall quickly to sleep. We each were in a dorm room with one roommate. I slept in a loft type bed set up, and my roommate slept in a regular bed across the room from me. That night around two in the morning I woke up out of a sound sleep to hear footsteps coming up the back stairs towards our room. I could not see anything because the room was pitch black. I heard the door to our room slowly open, and then I saw strange beings with big eyes come towards my bed. I was very frightened, so I did the only thing I could do, and that was to put my blankets over my head for protection. I thought this must be a dream. The next thing I saw were the blankets off me and a green beam of light going up from my stomach to my chest. It felt like it burned me, and then it was over. I looked over at my roommate to see where he was, and I tried to yell to him, but nothing came out. Finally with every bit of strength I had, I squeaked out, "Help!" He got up out of his bed, and I got out of mine. I told him what had just happened and that I needed his help. For the next hour he just held me as I shook. After a while I felt safe enough to go back to bed, and I fell back to sleep emotionally exhausted.

The next morning I told my mentor what I had experienced that night. He said, "Wow, whatever you opened up, you allowed "It" to come through to you. This is just what you needed." I felt pretty special that these beings came through to me. Whatever they did to me would have a lasting effect on the rest of my life.

The final night of the process we all had to take part in a play. I had to play a gay man. I got lessons from a gay man in our group. For the first time in my life, I was a gay man! I got to feel what being gay meant. It was not that bad in a controlled environment, but out in the real world I knew it had to be difficult to come out and admit that you were different than most, and would probably be negatively judged. It was a very eye-opening exercise and once again, that would have a lasting effect on my view of the world.

The 10-day process went by very quickly. I was sad to say good-by to everyone, but I was excited because one of the woman invited two other women and me to stay at her sponsor's mansion on Cape Cod. I had fun driving to the summer house, because I had not listened to the radio for almost two weeks. The music sounded great, and I felt a sense of relief that I was going to be staying with friends. We had been told not to go straight home, so that we could absorb all that we had been through. I was worried that I would be staying at our closed-up cottage in Mattapoisett for four days all by myself. Fortunately, this beautiful young woman took a liking to me and invited me to have fun with the others. The first night we were in the mansion, I was in awe of how luxurious their home was. We ate well, and even had a masseuse come over to personally treat each of us. I was worried I might get a boner in the middle of the session since she was a sexy blond rubbing me all over with oil and since I had been away from my wife for two weeks. We were told absolutely no sex during the Process and no sex during our time recuperating from the event. I had a beautiful bedroom to sleep in. I could not help but think that I might get a visitor in the middle of the night, and then what would I do?

The next evening we all were having fun playing ping-pong, when one of the women came down to play in just her nightgown. She was absolutely beautiful. I felt that this was a major test of my morals. I had a hard time not looking at her body through the almost see-through material that was barely hiding her bosoms. She knew I was interested in her, but I kept my wits about me and never made a move towards her. The next couple of days were fun, but we were all ready to get back to our real lives. I was very happy to begin my two-hour drive home. I could not wait to see Andrew, and make love to my wife.

HOME AGAIN ~

I walked into our house and saw Lisa in the kitchen. I was very happy to be home again after two weeks away. I was feeling very horny, and it did not take long for us to be in full embrace. At first I wanted to get a little kinky, but it did not take long to get right into normal business. It was a relief to be that close to her again. After making love, we went downstairs to have lunch. I was so happy to be able to play with Andrew. I really missed him. I was full of emotion, and wanted to tell Lisa everything I had been through. I became very weepy because my raw emotion was coming out. I said to her that she should really think about going when the next session of the Quadrinity Process was going to take place. She did not respond, but I knew this process would be life-changing for her. In fact it would be perfect for dealing with her history of incest. There had been others there that had been through what she had experienced, and they seemed to feel better, look better, and put the past behind them. The attendees appeared lighter, and full of self-love, which I believe was a long time coming for them.

My first assignment from the Process was to invite my parents over to tell them individually and face-to-face that I loved them and that I forgave them for anything that I had felt they had done to me as a child. I took each of them into the old room of our house and gave them each a long hug and cried with them. It felt like a very courageous thing to do and quite cathartic. I was relieved when this part of the Process was over.

Over the weekend I invited my best friend Fred to have dinner with us. He came over to find out more about what I had experienced. As I would tell of my experience, I would feel a wave of emotion come out of me. He was intrigued at what I told him, but he himself was not ready to take such a journey. I was glad though to tell him about it. Maybe in the future it might help him to go. I did not feel it was my duty to put pressure on him to go. If it was right for him, then he could make that decision himself. Lisa had also invited her best friend Robin to visit for a few days. At one point in a conversation I had with her, I said that the Process would be very helpful for Lisa to deal with her past history with her dad. Lisa asked her if she should go. Robin said no. I was dumbfounded. Here she had no idea what the Process was all about, and she was giving her naïve opinion on something I thought would change Lisa forever in a positive way. That was the last time I ever brought up the subject of the Hoffman Quadrinity Process. I was worried that if only one of us was working on getting better emotionally, how were we going to make it as a couple?

BACK IN THE SADDLE

It did not take long to get back into the normal swing of things at home. I played a lot with Andrew after work and enjoyed doing chores around the house. I had been away from work for two weeks, and then the Thanksgiving holiday break was only a few days away. It did not take me long to make appointments with existing insurance clients, as well as new ones. For the first time in a long time, I actually felt grounded and liking myself. I truly needed the break from daily life, and it could not have come at a better time. By letting go of my past, I was able to see the future more clearly and not be in such a rush to change the present. I knew that the Process had made a huge difference in my life, and I wanted to tell people that I cared about how it could help them. No one wanted to listen. I think they thought it was more like a cult, and that it was a weird thing to consider. I believe that most of my family and friends feared change and did not want to hear about it. I thought that it was better to keep it all to myself. I listened to the tapes that were given out at the end of the final day, and I wanted to keep the good vibe going. I think it was good for me and Lisa to take a mini vacation from each other. I was hoping that it would give her some perspective about her life and about us. She still seemed a little distant, but overall things felt better.

We spent all of 1993 doing new things. We hosted the first neighborhood bonfire. That winter there was over 120 inches of snow, so Andrew and I sledded a lot. We travelled back and forth to my grandmother's horse farm in Montpelier Vermont. Nannie Deane was very generous in giving out her paintings that she had made over the years. All one had to do was ask.

We also drove to Wilcox Pennsylvania to visit Lisa's family. It was an exhausting eleven-hour trip, but it was good for Andrew to meet his relatives, and for Lisa to reconnect with her cousins. It was during this visit that her aunt asked about her dad molesting her. Leslie had spilled the news to her younger sister, and the message spread throughout the family within hours. Her aunt tried to convince Lisa how much her dad loved her and the other kids. I was pissed that she offered no real comfort to what Lisa had experienced. The family wanted to kill her father, and at the same time did not know what really they could do. After that night of questioning, the subject of being molested only came up one more time with her cousin who was a social worker dealing with victims of abuse. I asked him what he was going to do. He said probably just stay away from her dad from now on. He could not believe that this had happened to his beautiful cousin. I wanted to say something regarding her family's denial, but I was outnumbered, and I knew that I could not change anyone's thinking. After four days with her family, I was very ready to get on the road and go back to Framingham.

CONVULSED ~

After we arrived back in Framingham after a long drive, I was very happy to be back in my safe place. I did not feel a sense of connection with her family. In fact, Lisa was very distant from me the entire time we were there. We had stayed in her father's vacation home, which was creepy. Most of the time we were visiting her family, so we did not have to spend too much time there. I noticed a little strange behavior from Lisa when we got back into the groove of things, but nothing I could really put my finger on. Not yet anyway. We had a scare one afternoon with her brother Danny when he showed up at our house with Leslie. He had been in court all day attending a hearing for his drunk driving charge and had not eaten anything. We all were sitting at the kitchen table, when all of a sudden he started making bizarre faces at Andrew. Danny's eyes began blinking rapidly. He then stood up. Lisa tried to put her arms around him asking what was wrong. He then fell into the edge of the kitchen counter while making guttural sounds. Blood and saliva was coming out of his mouth, and Lisa was moaning, "Please don't die!"

 I told Leslie to take Andrew out of the house away from this scary scene. I then called 911. The fire department was at our house in five minutes, then the police arrived a few minutes later. Danny began to come out of his convulsions, and actually sat up with the help of the medical technician. Everyone was relieved that he was ok. Lack of sleep, no food, inebriation, and stress were a recipe for disaster. Danny had dodged another bullet. All that he had was a big goose egg on his forehead from this incident. He was going to live for another day, but he never did remember this startling moment in his life. His brain just turned off the memory of his trauma, so that he could keep going without having to deal with his emotional and physical pain.

1994 was a year of change for my family. We learned that my brother Will and his wife Ellen were splitting up. I was sad to learn of this, but there was nothing I could do but be supportive of my brother and his kids. After that time, I have rarely spoken to her since for fear that it would appear that I was taking sides.

Not long after, we had a 90th birthday party in Vermont for my grandmother Nannie Deane at the Bolton Valley Ski resort. Will arrived with his two kids, but without Ellen. He appeared sad, but relaxed. I felt much less tense without her being around. All the great-grandchildren had fun playing together in the pool. It was a real honor to be part of my grandmother's milestone. John had written a song for her which I played the percussion on, and my cousin Tim presented her with a special proclamation from West Point allowing her to be buried next to her Conz. There was not a dry eye in the room.

MORE ALCOHOL

Lisa's alcoholism began to surface more and more. When we were driving down to Mattapoisett for our end-of-summer mini-vacation, she became quite amorous in the car. She kept trying to kiss me while I was driving. She kept putting her head down towards my lap. The only problem was that our son Andrew was in the back seat watching his mother act out of character. He knew something was not right and began to get agitated. I kept pushing her away. She finally stopped before we left the Stop and Shop parking lot in Framingham. After our hour-and-fifteen-minute trip to our family's cottage, we began to unload the car. I noticed a grey thermos by our bedside table. I knew it was not coffee, and I also knew the only time she became really horny was after a bout of drinking. I picked it up and brought it to her, and asked if she had been drinking? She did not give me a good answer. Only one that was very vague. She took the thermos away from me, and placed it back by the bed. After a few hours of playing with Andrew along the rocks down by the lighthouse, I put him down for his nap. Lisa came into the main part of the cottage, and began kissing me. She became sexually aggressive. It appeared that she enjoyed it, and so did I. It was weird though, because no other time had she asked for it that way. I did not know if she was letting her guard down due to the vodka she had just consumed or if she really wanted to experience something new to our love making. I knew the answer to this question, but I wanted to explore this exciting new passion further and thought I might never get this chance again. The down side was that what could she really experience inebriated? And would she even remember what we had done together? I was caught in my own dilemma—whether to focus on the desire to have this fantasy girl and great sex or whether to focus on her need to drink and the harm that it was doing to her body. I was having a real-life fantasy at the expense of possibly ruining our marriage. I truly hoped that my wife had as much fun as I had. Or was there also something else going on that I was not aware of? I felt a part of me had sold myself to the devil, but for now it felt really good being so physically close with Lisa.

A NEW SECRET

A few weeks later, after we had done our brief summer trips to Mattapoisett and Vermont, I accidentally over-stepped my boundaries with Lisa. I hit an emotional nerve that nearly ended our marriage. One day while I was sorting boxes in our attic and looking at all the cool stuff we had collected over the years since our college days, I came across a book that looked exactly like my journal book that I had written during my 82-day bicycle trip across the country. I wanted to skim through it since I had not seen it for many years. But when I opened it I noticed that the writing was not mine. I knew it was Lisa's journal, so I began to read from some of the pages. One page was detailing her relationship with her friend Bill, "That was very much the same as with dad". I did not read much further, because I felt awful that I was reading her personal diary, but at the same time I felt once again that she had not trusted me to discuss this painful ordeal in her life. I wanted a few days to get my courage up to tell her what I had uncovered, and maybe we could talk about it. I wanted to know what she had been feeling, and that I supported her. Maybe it would relieve some of the burden she was carrying all these years.

    A few days later I came into the living room where she was sitting and said, "I came across your diary upstairs. I thought it was my bicycle journal and I read a few pages." As soon as I revealed what I had done, I could feel the atmosphere in the room change dramatically. She looked at me in disbelief.

    "I can't believe you went through my personal stuff!" she exclaimed in a stunned tone.

    I told her that I wasn't snooping, and that I just wanted to know what she had been through. She was furious, and told me that she felt violated. I told her that she was blowing this way out of proportion, and that she could feel safe with me.

She would have none of it! She said that we were through, and that she did not want to be with someone that she could not trust. I regretted saying anything to her. I could not believe that something I had accidentally come across would end our marriage. Lisa walked out of the room, and I was left standing not knowing which way to turn. My dysfunctional relationship appeared to be over, all because I had opened my big mouth. Lisa barely spoke to me at dinner or in our bed. It felt as cold as ice lying next to her. I felt guilty and confused about opening the vault to a vast secret, and reinjuring an old wound. Another secret to deal with, but at the same time it did open up another door as to her reason for drinking. I was not looking at this as her dealing with a disease, but more of hurtful situations that triggered her need to escape or as she would often say, "self medicate".

I knew we could not handle this new crisis alone, so I suggested that we go back to the psychologists who could help sort out this anger safely and from an outsider's view. I was hoping that she would come around, but I was scared. I looked out the window the next morning and saw my brother John working in his yard, so I walked over to talk with him about this situation. Maybe he would have some sage advice. We went for a walk around the block, and I told him what I had uncovered—another secret. He listened, but did not give any advice, only his support.

I made an appointment with each of our psychologist to meet with us at the same time in Wayland. I felt a small glimmer of hope, because Lisa agreed to go with me. At this meeting, Lisa basically told them and me that she had had enough. I did not know what that meant. I said that I had accidentally come across her diary, and I was not trying to pry, but just to understand and support. I could see in their faces that they did not see much of a chance for saving this marriage.

I left the meeting feeling completely lost and deflated. During the next week I kept repeating that I would never look for anything personal of hers again, even though it was a "white lie". At this point I felt I had to protect myself from any new bombshell that was going to be dropped on me. Amazingly, I could see in her facial expression that she was beginning to loosen up. I thought this was an opportunity to ask if she would go one more time to our psychologist to discuss our situation. She agreed. At this session she acted completely differently. Her anger was gone. Both psychologists were stunned, and a little confused. How could someone go from abject hatred to acting as if nothing had ever occurred in less than a week? I thought this was crazy, and at the same time very manipulative. I felt that this was her way of saying, "back off or else". I did not want to go through the hell of a divorce, so I was willing to live with "crazy" rather than being out of the house and not having access to Andrew.

BABY #2

In October we learned that Lisa was pregnant with our second child. I guess all the drunken sex we had in Mattapoisett paid off. I truly believe that her inner clock was working overtime to have her need to procreate satisfied. I was more than happy to go along for the ride. I was very excited to have another child, and so was the rest of the family. Lisa's drinking seemed to subside due to the fact that she was carrying this precious child inside her. Once again I was in charge of keeping the family safe, which was a role I cherished. It also meant that for now I did not have to constantly worry about what new "situation" was going to present itself. The break was much appreciated, even if it was only going to be for nine months. I felt more relaxed, and we could focus on Andrew and have him get used to the idea that a brother or sister was on the way. He seemed to be excited. We took him to a class at the MetroWest Hospital that was focused on what he was to expect when his sibling arrived. I felt a major shift in our family dynamic, which felt very positive. I believed that Lisa's drinking was behind her and hopefully would not enter our family again.

Even though I saw no evidence of her drinking, there was a new problem—hoarding. Lisa liked to surf the Internet and buy things that had no intrinsic value to our family. The Fed Ex carrier made numerous trips to our house each week. At first I did not give it much thought, because the packages were small. But the problem became apparent when the packages kept coming. One package contained a small poster that was a signed copy of one of the original Munchkins from the Wizard of Oz. At first I thought this was kind of cool because Lisa had been in a local production of the Wizard of Oz where she played Dorothy. But she never displayed the poster. I never asked how much it cost. I was afraid to know. One day I came home where I learned that she had taken one of my grandfather's paintings that had hung in his office in Framingham for 70 years and that was an interesting western motif. She had an expert clean and tighten up the canvas, as well as replace the frame with a modern one. I was not happy that she did not discuss with me having this done to a tune of $400! We were living on one income, so I wanted to be conservative in our spending. Our builder who was working on replacing the exterior shingles of our house said that he was shocked as to how many times the Fed Ex truck arrived at our house. I said so was I!

A DIFFERENT NAME ∼

We put Andrew in a preschool program a few days a week in Bright Horizons to give Lisa a break and to ease her through the final months of her pregnancy. The days leading up to our baby's birth were filled with apprehension because we wanted her to have the baby the natural way, and not the painful recovery of a C-section. Luckily, the baby was not going to be as big as the nearly 10 pounds that had been Andrew's weight.

Lisa was due in early June, and her water broke on the eighth. She was not averse to taking the spinal or any other drugs that would help ease the searing pain. When the doctor performed the episiotomy, she did not feel anything. When the baby was pulled out of the birthing canal, we had a beautiful scrawny baby girl. We had agreed months before that if we had a girl, Emma would be her name, but she looked nothing like an Emma. She had long fingers and chicken legs. For almost a day she was our no-name baby. But for reasons I do not remember, we came up with Krista. It turned out to be the perfect name for her. From day one she was her own person. Feisty, and really did not like to be held. I knew she would be independent and confident throughout her life. I was ecstatic I had a girl!

During the next six months we continued to see our counselors, but less often than before. We just wanted to remain on an even keel while parenting two children. I even went on the drug Ritalin for a short period of time thinking it might help me concentrate better and improve my insurance career that was on a plateau. The drug made me feel like there was a 300-pound linebacker on my shoulders. Needless to say, I stopped taking it within a few days. I felt as though I was being manipulated by my alcoholic wife and the psychologist who enabled her. I was not impressed with any of them, but I was desperate to save my marriage and improve my income. The final time that Danny came down for Christmas Eve with Leslie, he was drunk and very angry. I tried to take a walk with him to sober him up and reduce the anxiety we all felt. I was very resentful that Leslie brought him down knowing that he was inebriated to ruin our Christmas. He became increasingly angry and gave the finger to passing cars on our street. I quickly took him back to our house and said there was nothing I could do. I wanted to take Leslie to the Lutheran Church midnight mass, but she knew that Danny was not going to get better soon, so she took him back to Fitchburg to spend Christmas day alone.

CREDIT CARD FRUSTRATION

My grandmother Nannie Deane gave us a very important Christmas gift, which she had been giving each of her grandchildren and children for the past several years. She gave us a check for $20,000. We were ecstatic over this monetary gift, because it would relieve us of our immediate cash flow issue.

My happiness was short-lived when I discovered the many credit cards that Lisa had opened and charged many miscellaneous objects on them. I was planning to use our gift to put away for a rainy day fund, as well as put towards the kids' college fund. But now my biggest financial fear was coming true...credit card debt along with their impossible high interest rates if you missed a payment. And because most of her purchases were through Ebay, it was nearly impossible to return what she had bought to recoup her payments.

One bill after another from different credit card companies came in the mail looking for payment. I was hurt, confused, and frustrated because I felt my grandmother's gift had been completely wasted on useless items, and once again created financial and emotional tension. I was hoping that our marriage would get better, but at what cost? My trust for my wife was nearing rock bottom, and I needed a solution to this mess. I tried to talk it out with Lisa, and try to reason with her to stop spending our money on crap that we were never going to use. I could see in her face that nothing was going to change. I was dealing with a financial enemy in my own home. I did not feel safe, and there was nothing I could do. I could not understand why she was trying to destroy us financially. Why bring our family down by way of spending away all of our savings, but do it in such a way that would bury us in debt? I wanted her to go back to work and repay all of what she spent, but in her alcoholic state of mind, that fantasy was never going to come true. I could not figure out if this behavior was a way to get back at her father for abusing her, or if it was self-hatred, or whether it was a way to get back at me for not understanding and for getting in the way of her drinking? There was no way out unless I threw away the computer, telephones, and was around her 24 hours a day. She continued to buy, and I was left with the decision of what to do next.

CUT UP CREDIT CARDS

One day I had decided that I was not going to be her financial victim any longer, so I went into her pocket book and found her credit cards. I was not sure which one I should tear up. She had three that I could find. There were probably more, but I was feeling weird going through her personal items. I took two, and cut them up hoping she would not notice them missing. I left one, so that she could use it for the basics like food. The next day she went to Stop and Shop to buy groceries with her mom. She came home later and said that she had to borrow money from her mom because she had lost the credit card she uses to buy food. I had cut up the wrong one. I left the one that had the largest interest rate, and now we owed her mother for the groceries! The following day, Lisa took my wallet because she wanted to use my American Express card to shop at Sears. When she came home, I asked her where my wallet was. She nonchalantly said she had left it at the store by mistake. I was beside myself, and said, "Shit!" I tore down Route 9 hoping that I might get there before my wallet was pilfered. Luckily the cashier had found it and held onto it before taking it over to lost and found. Nothing was missing, except my sanity!

STRAINED RELATIONSHIPS

As time went on, our relationship with my brother John and his wife Lynne became more strained. They saw Lisa's strange behavior up close. It was at their home next door that we were celebrating my parent's 40th wedding anniversary along with my grandmother Nannie Deane. It had been a few years since Pop Deane had died. The four of them began dating during the summer of 1951. My grandmother lost my grandfather during WW II after he had been captured on Corregidor by the Japanese. Deane Davis's wife died of cancer not long after. A few years later he had discovered my grandmother was available and working in Boston, so he pursued her at the same time my father had seen my mother while playing tennis in Mattapoisett. In fact Deane Davis said to my father, "If you marry Patsy, I'll marry Marjorie!" On July 5th 1952 they were married four hours apart in Boston.

During the anniversary party that night with my brothers and sister in laws and children, we enjoyed each others' company during dinner. But it was after dinner while Lisa and Lynne were in the kitchen cleaning up that Lisa began bad-mouthing the family. I heard about it later from my father. I never did understand it, except that Lynne said that she would never trust Lisa—ever! I thought that was rather extreme, and so the neighborly relationship was forever strained.

CLU

During this stressful time dealing with my dysfunctional home, I tried to instill some normalcy by focusing on my insurance practice of more than 10 years. I enjoyed meeting new people, and creating insurance plans to solve problems for my clients. I worked on passing the 10 course CLU program with my mentor from work. He grilled me on the days we were together at his condo in Winchester Massachusetts with the same questions I had read and studied the weeks before we met. The hard work paid off, and I was able to pass three exams. But as the focus of studying was steered more toward my wife's crazy unsafe behavior, I could not pass the fourth exam. Even after two retakes, I came within 10 points of passing, but could not crack the 70 percent barrier. I was frustrated and wanted to pass so badly. I did not like giving up, and I did not like failing, but my mind was elsewhere. I had to put all of my energy into my business, so I could make a living, and most importantly into my family, so that I could be there for them. I knew that until I removed the Pink Elephant from our house, I would not be able to move forward.

Lisa's drinking was usually out of sight. Once in a while she would let her guard down, and not notice that she had left a bottle in a conspicuous place like her dresser drawer. One day I came across a Vodka bottle. I waited until she had blacked out on our bed, then I brought her mother up and showed her the bottle. Once again I stepped right into a mine field. I thought Leslie would understand and possibly give me some advice as to what to do with her drunk daughter. Leslie went right into attack mode and said that I was responsible for getting Lisa into rehab. What I really was looking for was some moral support, not aggression or blame. From that point on I knew Leslie was clueless and that she would only hinder my ability to help her daughter. Her role had always been the family enabler, and there was no way to change her. She held the key to the great family cover up. If one secret was revealed, then ten more would come spewing out, and she would have to be held accountable for not protecting her kids from the sexual predator. I was finally seeing the truth, and worse I was in this fight alone and very vulnerable.

KEEP OUT

Another subset of Lisa's disease was not just the financial devastation, but the increasing isolation. When we did have friends over for dinner or a simple get together, Lisa was already inebriated. She would slur her words or act silly. Friends felt strange being around her. They could sense something was amiss, and my feeling tense and embarrassed did not help the situation. Lisa liked to put me down behind my back. She was like the stealth alcoholic. Her acid tongue flew under my radar, but was seen as odd by our friends. Our house was becoming more and more a trash pit. Every room downstairs on the first floor was becoming more cluttered with furniture and stuff that she liked to buy when she had too much time on her hands. I tried to clean up when I could, but I never had enough time to do a really thorough job of it. During the weekends I tried to fit in plenty of time with Andrew and Krista playing outside having fun, and also putting in some time to clean up the ever-growing mess. As time went on, we no longer entertained except for the occasional birthday party. The reality was the alcoholism was taking over our family.

GREEN-UP DAY ~

During a visit to my Nannie Deane's Morgan Horse farm I came across a large flag neatly folded in my grandfather's office closet. I recognized the words "Green Up" in green and white lettering. This flag symbolized his very successful state-wide clean-up effort back in April 1970. I had been asked by a friend to come up with something that would be meaningful and effective for the town's 300th birthday, and I knew immediately that this was the answer. I was volunteering to help the largest town in America clean up before the festivities were to begin in just two years. My grandmother said that I could take the flag, so that I could sell the town officials on the idea of a town-wide clean up event.

After a few months of time and negotiation, I got the OK to move forward. I spoke to my attorney friend to create a 501(C)(3). He agreed to do it Pro Bono. The name of it was going to be GreenUp, Inc. I now could solicit businesses and friends to give money and services to help pay for the t-shirts, gloves, and trash bags. The town was about to receive its best clean up in 300 years! I was pleased how quickly GreenUp Day was coming together. My co-founder, who I had teamed up with, was able to tap into his town official contacts to help with any road blocks that might get in the way. We focused on the Boys and Girls Scouts, as well as large businesses in the area like Staples and Adessa to help with monetary donations and volunteers to actually do the cleaning up.

We chose the last Saturday in April 1998 to kick off the event. The local newspapers were all over it. Going green was all the new rage, so this was the right program at the right time. I was spending a great deal of time with the logistics and delegation of GreenUp Day, while trying to juggle my family and business obligations. As a Libra, I was able to balance all of my activities including coaching Andrew's soccer team. The one thing I had let slide was Lisa's increasing drinking problem. I needed a diversion from her craziness, while focusing on something positive and wonderful. I was not sure why her drinking was becoming more severe. Was it due to her past or was it her need to keep me drawn into her drama? Either way I remained focused on GreenUp Day and the hundreds of volunteers that had committed to making it a great success.

The first Framingham town-wide cleanup event was a huge success with thousands of volunteers cleaning up tons of trash. There was no mishap of any kind, which helped to promote the next year's event. The press gave wonderful reviews, and I felt all the time I had spent had been worth it. The only downer was Leslie yelled at me for not caring what was happening to her daughter. That truly upset me, because there was not a whole lot more I could do except be supportive if she accepted going to treatment. I was not able to control her drinking. I had tried in a variety of ways to help, all of which had failed. I needed support, but I knew I would never receive it from her immediate family. In the end it was going to be every man for himself. I began slowly to understand the disease a little more.

THE JONESES

There was one thing that kept rearing its ugly head, and that was trying to keep up with the "Joneses". Lisa was constantly comparing our family with John and Lynne's next door. I did not care if they had more money or a bigger house, but Lisa did. All I wanted was for our families to get along so that our kids could have fun playing together. Lisa had other ideas. It felt like a competition where one did not exist. I knew that she was jealous of my semi normal family compared to what she had grown up in. I was not able to change the way I was raised, nor did I want to try. She wanted to change and fix me, which would give her more control of us. The wedge was widening between our families, but all I wanted was a peaceful existence and to relax in my own home. I did not feel as though there was anything I could do, because if I did what she wanted me to do, I would lose myself, as well as my self respect. The reality from the street was very different from what was really going on. We looked like an all American family, but truly our family was in real trouble. And the more I tried to keep up with this façade, the more of a mess I made for me and my kids.

RAM

When tensions were high, I tried my best to divert the attention that was on us by acting childish or taking physical risks with my life. I never put my kids at risk, but at the same time they witnessed my bizarre behavior. The way I did this was easy. Our next door neighbor had a small sheep farm. The fenced in paddock abutted our yard, and in that paddock was a ram along with the other sheep. My son Andrew and I would daily go out in the yard and kick the soccer ball to each other, but more often than not an errant pass would be kicked into the paddock alongside the 300-pound ram. I then would have to figure out a way to retrieve the ball without getting head-butted in the rear. I was usually able to jump the fence, run to the ball, and climb back over the fence with the ball. But one late afternoon the ball once again found its way into the paddock.

I looked down into the field to see just how far away the ram was, so that I could get to the ball. He was a good 30 feet away, so I decided to go for it. I slowly climbed over the fence, and then dashed to the ball that was in the center of the paddock. As I turned with the ball, I could hear the ram begin to charge. I began to get nervous, and as I ran I tripped over a rock and fell face first into the muck. I could feel the earth tremble with the ram coming straight for me. I waited for the inevitable strike of his head, but felt nothing except its hot breath in my ear. He was so surprised that I was just lying there that he put his nose down to smell me, and then turned and walked back towards the field. I was very happy that the ram had not rammed me for I had seen my nephew Sid get butted and fly in the air! I had dodged a huge bullet, but my reputation was being damaged with each immature move I made. I was being watched.

Another misstep on my part was one snowy day our next door neighbor's son was down by our brook with his sister. I was walking down the street towards our house with Andrew and Krista. There was snow and chunks of ice along the side of the road above the stream left by the snowplow. He was trying to hide behind the trees from us, while yelling at me to throw an ice ball at him. So without thinking I picked up a chunk of ice and threw it at the tree he was hiding behind 20 feet away. It was perfect shot. The ice splattered against the tree in all directions. Unfortunately at that moment his head appeared to the side of the tree, and the ice hit him in the face and cut him on his cheek. He began to cry. I immediately ran to him, and brought him into my house to check him out. It was not a deep wound, and a bandage was all that was needed. I asked him if he was OK, and he said he was, and I sent him home with his sister. I thought nothing more of it, and in my mind no big deal, except I did not call his parents to let them know what had happened. When he arrived home, his parents were entertaining John and Lynne and other friends of theirs. They were disturbed to see his puffy face, red eyes, and cut on his cheek. The father asked what happened. He told them that I had hit him with an ice ball. Of course they were furious with me. I could have diffused the situation by walking over with him to explain, but I did not think it was that big a deal. It was. I learned about it from John the next day. I told him how things actually turned out, but it did not matter. Once again my reputation was tarnished, and this time it involved a neighbor's son. The neighbors did not talk to me after that. I did write them an apology note, but my relationship with them was never the same.

The following weekend I was up on my roof over the kitchen shoveling off the most recent snow that had piled up. I was always worried that too much snow would someday cave in on us. My nephew Sid and our next door neighbor's son climbed up the ladder to see what I was doing. I let them come up just for a few minutes to experience the view, and then told them they had better get down or something might go wrong. My nephew Alex who was Andrew's age was at the bottom of the ladder looking up. I told him that he could climb up just to see what they had seen. He climbed to the top of the ladder and put both feet on the roof, and then decided to get back down.

The next words out of his mouth were, "I can't wait to tell mommy we were on the roof!"

"You better not!" I half jokingly said."

Once again I could feel in my gut impending doom. That night while eating dinner Alex blurted out, "I was on Uncle Tom's roof today!"

Sid then said, "Alex, you know Uncle Tom told you not to say anything!"

It was another nail into the relationship coffin between us. Each time I interacted with any kids in the neighborhood I was now a marked man. So I made the decision not to play with them anymore and to keep a very low profile. I was embarrassed that it come to this point, but now I was forced to completely focus on my own family and our difficulties. I had tried so hard to divert attention away from my family that I had done just the opposite. Now no matter what I did right or wrong, I was labeled.

INDEPENDENCE

I was very fortunate to have a career selling life insurance that allowed me the independence to be home whenever I needed to be. I also was able to give some of the care-taking of my children to their grandmothers. Although I never really felt good about Krista going off with Leslie because she would often take her to visit her alcoholic Uncle Danny at his disheveled apartment in Fitchburg. I never knew what he was capable of doing when he was inebriated. I did know that he was a very angry drunk, so that did not make me feel comfortable that my daughter was in his presence. I learned later that Leslie had also taken her to visit her pedophile grandfather. I could not believe that she was that naïve or stupid to bring her to a family known predator! So I put a stop to having Krista go with her any longer. I came to realize that all I was doing was enabling Lisa to drink by having her mother relieve her of her parental responsibilities.

Now all I had were my parents who lived up the road and my brother John who I knew I could rely on if things got really bad. I found myself home a lot more so that I could spend more time protecting my kids by getting them out of the house to play. Andrew was showing signs that he really liked to play soccer and basketball, so I gladly spent the time kicking and shooting. I also got the opportunity to coach his U10 soccer team. Most kids started much younger, but I had my hands full with parenting two kids, and grappling with an alcoholic, so there had not been time to do much else. I found that it did not take as much time as I had thought to keep 10 kids actively engaged for two hours. All I had to do was have a practice planned a few days in advance. One of the mothers said she was amazed at the amount of time I gave to the kids especially at four o'clock on a week day afternoon. She was sure that I was a stay at home dad. As I got to know her better I let her in on the family secret. At that point she understood my predicament.

I found that preparing for practices and coaching at the intramural games was the perfect distraction for me at a time when I felt as though I had very little control over my life. I coached both fall and spring soccer and had the summer off. This was the time that it gave me a break, and we could go down to Mattapoisett. As time went on, that too became more stressful, because Lisa and I were in close quarters, and going to the beach and being land-locked was making it less fun to be together. Our stays were now only for weekends and no longer.

DOING MORE ~

Looking back it may have been the more prudent decision to remain at 19 Church Street in my grandparent's home with far fewer financial worries, but I did enjoy living next to John and Lynne, and their two sons Sid and Alex. It was great to see all four of our kids playing together, although Sid liked to beat up on his younger brother when his parents weren't looking. I tried to explain to Lynne what was going on, but she believed I was a terrible parent for what I allowed to continue in my house, and was not about to listen to anything I was going to say. What I learned in Al-Anon is that if you point your finger at someone you have three pointing right back at you!

John and I continued recording songs that he wrote. I had bought a Yamaha DTX electronic drum set. This allowed us to play silently without disturbing his sleeping kids after nine o'clock at night. We also played hockey on Monday nights together at Loring Arena just a few miles away. So I was able to get some time away from my stressful home. The difficult part was walking back into the emotionally dead house. Lisa was already in bed by eight o'clock, so I knew when I came back there was only going to be silence and loneliness. I rarely fell asleep before eleven and was up by six to get the kids up and ready for school.

I also had recently joined the gym that Lisa had joined partly because I wanted to get in better shape, but also because I did not trust Lisa. I believed that if the opportunity arose with one of the hot men working out there she would not have the mental defenses to turn down the invitations. I found while I was working out there women would flirt and come up to me to talk, and possibly want more. I never strayed, but it was great to feel appreciated and attractive. I knew it would just add to the pain I was already feeling. I did not need to add guilt into the mix.

The paint on the exterior of our house began to peel again even after we had recently had the house completely painted. It was not the fault of the paint or the painter. It was a moisture issue, and the cedar shingles were old and needed to be replaced. We decided to take the drastic measure to remove all the shingles, to make sure the house was properly insulated, and then to replace the old shingles with ones that would be dipped in primer on both sides to prevent this problem from ever happening again. Our contractor George gave us a price of $19,000 to do everything. He found a painter who he felt was reliable, and so we agreed to his estimate. After the shingles were removed and the Tyvek insulation was installed, the process of tacking- up the new double dipped shingles was a slow process to complete. Because we lived in a historic district, we were not allowed to change the configuration of the house without permission of the board. It would have been far easier and less expensive just to put up long boards, but it would have taken away the English Cottage look of the house. We did get approval for one change to make the front door entryway a foot larger in height to allow for a screen door to be installed. That took weeks to get approval, and did add to our costs, but it was a good decision. The new door gave us a little more protection from the outside world both in safety and in heat loss prevention.

GRAVE SITE ~

One day we invited my parents over for lunch to have them see their grandchildren, but before they arrived Lisa and I had an argument. She was drunk again, and she threatened to throw a cutting board at me. I knew that getting into it with her was not going to end well, so I decided to leave the house for a while to let the situation cool down and her to sober up. I always felt comfort when I walked up our road to the Edgell Grove Cemetery to where my Greeley grandparents and Aunt Lulu were buried. They had all passed away a few years before, all at about the same time, and they were all in their 90's. It felt good to commiserate with them, so I walked over to their grave site that over looked the Massachusetts Turnpike. I asked them for help, because I did not know what to do. I thought that if I left my problem in their hands maybe, with the help of their fellow angels, they might bring on a miracle. I felt better after 20 minutes, so I walked back to our house feeling a little less burdened.

As I got closer to the house, I saw my parents' car in the driveway. I was really curious to find out what was going on. I walked in to find everyone smiling and chatting away. I did not try to understand, and more importantly my prayers had been answered for now.

We had lunch as if nothing was wrong, but I felt as though I was living in a never-ending lie, and that no one could see through this charade. Later, when I was speaking to my father about what had occurred, he said that he thought something was strange when I was not there to greet them. That discussion made me feel that maybe the outside world was beginning to catch on. If Lisa could be this crazy unapproachable tyrant one minute and then the next be all smiles, who was going to show up when she was alone with my kids? I found that she was more agitated when her disease felt threatened. I was trying to put light on a very dark secret. I was never sure what my next move should be, because I knew I was taking an emotional risk any time I tried to communicate with her. How could this 5'1" woman from an insane family carry so much power and fear? I also found the more I intervened the more I got in the way of natural consequences from taking care of things. But fear makes one do crazy things. I was going to learn the hard way.

AFTERGLOW ~

One night after we made love, I noticed a greenish glow halo around Lisa's face. I had seen the glow only two times before, once when Andrew was conceived, and the next, Krista. I saw that my Trojan had broken. I was a little concerned because I knew that Lisa did not want any more children and that it was not the most responsible thing to do at this time of emotional crisis. I did not say anything to her the next morning fearing that she would get angry, and also I thought it was a one in a million chance that she would get pregnant by one faulty condom accident.

About a month later in late March of 1999, Lisa was complaining to her friend Angela that she was not able to drink coffee because it was making her queasy. Angela said, "Oh my God...you're pregnant!" Lisa came home from the drug store with a pregnancy test kit. Reluctantly she went to the bathroom to find out if it was true. The blue stripe appeared. She was pregnant. I was thrilled to be having another child, but Lisa not so much. I felt a bit guilty, because I knew what had happened and had given her no warning. Once again, Lisa was able to get pregnant with very little effort. Back in October just six months earlier, Lisa had a short-term miscarriage, which we were not prepared for, but there was almost no emotional trauma because it happened so early on, and we were not trying to have another child. I was not thinking clearly or maturely, because I was infatuated with the idea of having another baby to hold and love. The other kids were growing up so quickly that I really wanted one more child to add light to our family. But the truth of the matter was that Lisa had not conquered her drinking problem, far from it, so this child was going to cause a bit more stress in our relationship whether I liked it or not.

We waited a month before telling anyone outside of our home just to make sure Lisa and the baby were going to be OK. One day at work, I said to my father out of the blue that if we have a son, we are going to name him Robert Stiles after my grandmother's younger brother who was a World War I flying ace shot down while flying over Germany in a biplane. My father came into my office with a very sullen face just shaking his head back and forth. He was not happy with the news, because he knew just how difficult the situation was now, as well as dangerous. My uncle and aunt were visiting our office, and they were thrilled with the news, but they really did not understand the gravity of my situation.

Word spread quickly throughout my family, and the feedback was concerned congratulations. I was hoping that Lisa would be forced to get her act together, and absolutely could not drink while she was pregnant. For the next nine months, I saw no signs of her drinking. I thought the old habit was a thing of the past, and now our family would be healthy once again. During the summer months while we swam at our neighborhood pool, I enjoyed watching Lisa's belly get bigger in her bathing suit. It was very exciting to know that she was carrying this precious being inside her for the world to see. I was very happy and excited for things to come. The baby was due in early November, and for me that day could not come soon enough. The time passed quickly, and there was no weirdness to be felt. I think the attention that Lisa received was very positive for her, and the kids and I spent a lot of time playing outdoors, which gave her time to rest and to not be too stressed out, plus the grandparents were always a phone call away. The anticipation was coming to a climax, and soon our family would be complete.

VASECTOMY ~

On October 3rd my 40th birthday arrived, and so I decided to have a vasectomy. This was the perfect time to do it, because I knew that once Lisa and I had sex again anything was possible. Since condoms were no match for me, I knew this kind of procedure would do the trick. Since my brother John had it done a few years prior, I was feeling OK about it. My primary care physician gave me the name of Doctor Dick whose office was located near the MetroWest Hospital. I called his office and they gave me an appointment for the following week. When I arrived at his office I began reading all the pamphlets on what was to come. If I had any second thoughts, I was hoping that the doctor would help dispel them. As I spoke to Doctor Dick he was both matter of fact and calming with each question I asked him. Since I had no more questions or any objections, he began to look at his schedule.

"It doesn't look like I have anything open for a few months," he said. "Oh, here's an opening next Wednesday!"

Yikes, I was at first glad that I could put this off for a while, and then I went right into fear mode.

The doctor said that he looked forward to seeing me again, and oh by the way, the doctor that was going to assist him was Doctor Dagger. Doctor Dick and Dagger, so now I know the universe has a sense of humor! The week went by very quickly, and soon I found myself in the hospital with my legs up in stirrups, and two large nurses cracking jokes about the position I had put myself in. They took my blood pressure as standard procedure, and it was high.

One of the nurses said, "I thought you were a brave man?"

"Yea," I replied, "I feel like a scared turtle!"

After Doctor Dick stuck two large needles into my ball sack, I felt nice and numb. As he worked on my family jewels, he made the statement, "If you are ever thinking about having this procedure reversed...don't even try."

At that moment I knew he was good. After the surgery was completed, I was able to drive myself home. I felt very little pain. Except for those two horrible needles, the whole experience was not that bad. But I knew after this baby, there would be no more babies made from me. I was told that I had to come back to the hospital to check my sperm count to make sure that everything was working as planned, and that those little suckers were not making their way through any of my tied off tubes. So after the romantic ritual of cumming into a sterile hospital jar, I brought my love-making potion down to the MetroWest Medical facility for one last examination. I asked the main receptionist where was I supposed to bring my sample? She pointed me down the hall to another office. When I got there, they did not know what I was to do with it. I finally brought the jar to the office where I had the procedure. The woman behind the desk told me that this was not the place to bring it to either, so I decided to go home and take my chances.

ROBERT STILES

On November 1st 1999, I arrived home from work around 5:00 to be greeted with the news that Lisa's water had broken. Andrew and Krista were playing downstairs, and they felt the excitement and urgency in us. While Lisa went upstairs to pack her day clothes and necessities, I called my parents to tell them it was time. They arrived within 20 minutes, and Lisa and I were on our way back to MetroWest Hospital. We knew what to expect, and were fairly calm driving. This time it was going to take some time for our baby to enter the world. The nurses took us right up to the birthing room, which felt like a nice hotel. I truly enjoyed this moment in our lives, because the energy and love was almost intoxicating for me. I felt as though everything was in order. I knew my place in the world as a loving father, and Lisa was the grounded and stable mother. Lisa was given the necessary drugs to negate any pain, so all she had to focus on was pushing. The slow process went through the night into the following day. It was not until three in the afternoon that we felt progress was being made. It was at that point that the nurses began to get excited, and yell "Push!" Lisa grimaced and gave it her all.

Baby came out soon after. He was indeed a boy. Robert Stiles, who had waited nearly 80 years to reappear out of our family history, was here to make his own destiny. He was taken to the baby station, and Lisa was tended to make sure all her vital signs were normal. She once again was amazing. I was so excited that I could not wait to call all the grandparents. Grandma Leslie came down the next day with Danny who was once again soused and unpleasant. He was jealous that once again his sister came through, and he was all messed up. I felt very put upon, because I was left with the responsibility of taking him out of the room, and walking him around the hospital to help sober him up. He was once again a disruption to our joyous occasion, and Leslie left me once again with her family mess. Luckily they were gone within a few hours, and then my parents arrived with Andrew and Krista. We allowed them to hold their baby brother for the very first time while sitting in the big chair in our room. Just like the others, Robert was as bald as a cue ball with a smattering of peach fuzz.

Because we had arrived at the hospital so late, we were allowed to stay an extra day, which would help Lisa heal from her minor surgery. I had planned to take a few days off from work to help get the house clean and ready for Lisa and baby. I made a bed out of the downstairs futon, so that Lisa would not have to climb the stairs when I was not home. I really enjoyed staying home with the kids for a few nights. I wanted them to feel special. The following day it was time to bring Robert home. His room and crib were all set, but the only premature move we had made was selling all the baby furniture the year before at our neighborhood yard sale never imagining having another child. So whatever money we had made went right back into buying a new baby swing and pen. Leaving the hospital was a real let down. There we felt like royalty, but now going back into the real world was going to be difficult with three kids. Driving home Lisa and I hardly spoke because we were exhausted. Pulling into our driveway we were greeted with a single congratulations baby boy balloon. There was no hoopla or family to welcome us home. Everything felt different. The joy and adrenaline had passed through us, and now it was just us. I felt like I had snuck one by the goalie, but I had been called for being in the crease.

UNEASY FEELING

It was exciting having another baby in the house because Andrew and Krista were old enough to go places like the park or could walk to the Framingham Centre Common to kick a soccer ball. It was easy for me to look after two mobile kids who were potty trained and to allow Lisa the time to focus on Robert. The first time I saw her breast-feed him on the futon I was very much at ease knowing she was going to be a wonderful mother to him. It appeared all the crazy alcoholic behavior was behind us once and for all. She had beaten her demons and I was very proud of her.

I was trying not to fool myself, but that uneasy feeling way down deep was still there no matter how hard I tried to ignore it. For now my best distraction was my work, my kids, and the holidays that were going to be a blast with a new baby to show off. I would be damned if I was going to let this feeling screw up my family. I had it all under control. During Christmas Nannie Deane, Robert's great-grandmother, got to hold him for the first time. I was in awe that the matriarch of the family was actually holding a fourth generation. I was so inspired. His Aunt Lynne loved holding him, so all was right and at peace with the world for now. I really believed that now with three kids there was no time to mess things up. Family came first and the rest would just have to wait their turn. With the new millennium about to begin, the world was about to go through a big change whatever that was. The fear was that because the year 2000 was coming that many things would not work and that planes would fall from the sky and the calendar would be all messed up. When the ball dropped in Times Square I took a deep breath and waited. Nothing happened. The digital clock lighted up to 12:01 just as it should. The new millennium was here with no sign of trouble. I was relieved that there was going to be no interruption in my business life and that there was going to be no increase in traffic jams. It turned out that most of it was hype by the press basically to sell papers and ad space on TV. The network execs got the play that they wanted, but at what cost?

AGENCY'S PARTY

Our first holiday party of the year was held at the Royal Sonesta Hotel in Boston and was hosted by the insurance agency I worked for in Wellesley. We were invited along with 30 other insurance agents and their wives. We were to go with my mother and father in one car to make it convenient for all of us. We liked these types of parties because the food and drinks were free, and the attendees were fun to talk to. When we arrived at the parking garage I noticed that Lisa was acting a little goofy. She kept sighing, and saying, "Oh oh", because this was the first time she had been away from our new baby. We had a well qualified baby sitter to look after all three kids, so I did not understand what her concern was for being allowed to get away for a few hours and enjoy herself. It had been about a year since I saw her act this way. She was over-smiling and her eyes looked glazed over, and her face was red. I knew what this meant, and I was very concerned. I did not know how I could cover up for her erratic behavior around my working associates. I was hoping for a positive outcome, but not expecting one.

When we arrived at the party I naively went to the bar to bring her a glass of wine thinking that this might calm her down, but this one attempt on my part was like throwing gas on an open flame. Sitting down next to us was one of the newer agents that had recently joined our agency. I had been doing some joint work with him, and I thought he was an overall good guy. Lisa took an immediate liking to him and put her arms around him, while making suggestive remarks out loud for the table to hear. He looked very uneasy, and so I quickly made sure that she let go of him. It made for a very awkward moment, and I knew I would hear about it the next time I saw him in the agency.

A young secretary from our agency who had a crush on me came up to our table to say hello. Lisa whispered, "She's pretty". I had nothing to say, because I was not interested. I was upset that Lisa was drunk, and I was sure everyone noticed, but no one ever let on. I was relieved that either they were unaware that my wife had a drinking problem, or they were being polite on my account. All night long Lisa sweated and smiled. I made sure that she did not have another drink, but by that time it was much too late. Fortunately the night came to an end for us by 11:00, and my parents dropped us off at our home in Framingham. All was fine at home. The kids were asleep, and soon so was Lisa.

After the baby sitter left, I stayed up a while longer just thinking what had transpired this night. I was very worried that her drinking had begun so soon after Robert was born, and I knew what was coming. But this time I now had three kids to worry about, including a new baby. I thought, how was I going to be able to concentrate on work, and at the same time have people come into my house to keep an eye on Lisa? I felt that this was very unfair, and almost an impossible situation to be in. But I would figure out a way. I now had to also parent a fourth child, but one who had a mental addiction. Here was a child disguised as an adult, and one who was very clever in manipulating people. I had to work out a plan that would enable me to ward off any future disaster, because it was inevitable that it was coming.

NEW MINISTER

The next day was Sunday, so we went to our Unitarian church that was just down the road from our home in Framingham Centre. The new minister was going to give her first sermon of the New Year, and I was happy to be going to a safe place with my family. The minister was a very attractive young woman who had a no-nonsense way about her. She was very confident, and had been an important source of comfort after my father's heart attack. She gave a sermon that was not preachy but right from the heart. The church had always been a place where I felt I could be me. I had been known to cry at the moment of sharing, especially after informing the congregation that my brother-in-law Devon had passed away. I had dealt with more than one personal tragedy, but the love from the church members helped to guide me through. I wanted to build a relationship with the minister, so that I could trust her enough to let her in on my family secret. She already knew the rest of my extended family and was in awe of the Greeley mystique surrounding their involvement of the church both financially and spiritually.

It did not take long to build that relationship. I think she had known about some of the troubles we were going through from my mother. I needed another trusted ally, and I chose the right one. Because I now knew that Lisa had gone back to her old alcoholic ways, and I felt alone and discouraged. I was naively hoping that having Robert would help stabilize our relationship and once and for all do away with the awful disease. Just the opposite occurred.

When I went back to work on Monday the new agent that Lisa had made the moves on told me that he had felt very uncomfortable with her pawing all over him. I apologized and told him what was going on. He kind of understood, but I could feel the tension between us. Not long after this incident he found that the business of selling life insurance too much to handle financially and quit.

I now had both eyes open, and watched for signs of her drinking. There were times when all was fine at home, and then others when her face appeared red and her actions were goofy. I now never knew what to expect when I came home. The wintertime was fun because we had lots of snow for sledding down our small hill on the north side of our property. Andrew and Krista loved sliding down the hill with their snow tubes and snowboard. We also had our annual neighborhood bond fire that was usually started by a hefty amount of gasoline and old dismantled Christmas trees that went up in a blaze of glory. I did my best to keep the outside world at bay hoping they would believe that we were a very normal family. I was feeling a great deal of pressure that all eyes were on our every move, so that I was under pressure to keep the peace. Lisa did not want anyone to know the truth, and felt as though she was on the hot seat. When someone got to close with their eyes this was just another reason to self medicate.

MATTAPOISETT SCARE ⁓

I did not realize just how much Lisa had begun to drink again until the day we decided to go to Mattapoisett to open up the cottage early in April 2000. We had planned to take our two vehicles—the minivan and the sedan—so that we could bring all the kids' stuff as well as the extra blankets, lamp shades, and curtains that needed to be put up. That Friday I came home from work early to help pack up for our trip and to help Lisa out so it was not all on her shoulders. By the time we were ready to go about 2:00 Robert was still taking his afternoon nap. We did not want to wake him, but the other kids were very excited to get on the road, so Lisa and I agreed to split up and go at different times. I asked her if she felt comfortable driving down to Mattapoisett alone with Robert since she had never driven there on her own. She said that she would be fine, and that it was OK to take the kids now rather than have them wait any longer. We could also do some food shopping before they arrived later in the afternoon.

I made sure that she knew it was very easy to get to the cottage. All she had to do was go Route 9 west, to 495 south, all the way to exit 1 onto Route 195, and then finally to exit 19A to Mattapoisett. She said she would be fine, and that I did not have to worry. So we left. Before I left I called my parents to let them know what we were doing, and asked them to check up on Lisa later that afternoon just to make sure she was sober. They agreed, and I felt fine about leaving. At that time we had no multiple cell phones, so I needed a way to keep tabs on her before she was leaving, that way I would have some time reference. The drive would not take more than an hour and twenty minutes, and it was a safe and easy drive with very few exit changes.

Andrew, Krista, and I arrived at the cottage in the middle

of the afternoon and unloaded the minivan. We put the house together and then went down to the beach for a quick swim. Later we drove to Stop & Shop and bought our food for the weekend. We ate dinner around 6:00, and did not wait for Lisa and Robert to show up, because we thought they would be getting off to a late start. By 7:30 it was time to begin thinking about bedtime for the kids. Lisa and Robert had not arrived yet. I figured that they had waited until after dinner to hit the road, so I was not worried. By 8:30 I had laid down with the kids to help them go to sleep by telling them stories and having fun just talking. I woke up at 10:30 in a panic. There was no Lisa and no Robert in the house. They had not arrived yet. The kids woke up too knowing that something was very wrong. I looked around the house to make sure maybe they had not come in and slept in another bedroom. They had not. I called my parents to find out if they had seen Lisa off. My father said that they had gone over around 5:00 to make sure they were going and that Lisa looked alright. My dad said that they left soon after they had gone over.

    So where were they? I asked my parents to go by the house to see if the car was still in the driveway and if they still were at home. They called me back about 20 minutes later and said that her car was not in the driveway. Now I was really in a panic. I then called the state police to find out if there had been a report of an accident involving a Nisan Altima. The dispatcher told me there had not been any reports of any accidents this evening. I was relieved, but at the same time very worried. Where were they? My head told me to go out and look for them, but my gut said to do just the opposite. How would I ever find them? I did not know what roads they had taken, and because she did not own a cell phone at that time I could not call her. So I decided to stay in the cottage with the kids. They knew something was very wrong, so we just sat on the couch in the living room and remained in our dozed panic. I got up a few times to walk around, because I was so restless, and at the same time I tried not to alarm the kids anymore than they already were.

At about 11:30 p.m. we heard the breezeway door open. They had arrived safely!

"Someone changed all the road signs going south on Route 495." That's the first thing Lisa said.

"That's strange," I replied, "all the signs looked the same to me."

The kids and I were very relieved. But at the same time I was very confused. Where had she driven for the past 6 hours? I was too tired to ask, and really wanted the children to get back to sleep, so I waited until the next morning to ask.

The morning came fast, and I was up by 7:00. Andrew and I drove to Dunkin Donuts which was our morning ritual when we came to Mattapoisett. An hour or so later everyone was up, so I decided to ask Lisa what route did they take? She said that she had gotten confused and just kept driving. She did not know where she was, so finally she pulled over after a few hours of driving somewhere near the Bourne Bridge. I could not understand how she could get lost since we had been driving the same route for the past 10 years. I also noticed that the oil light was on in the dashboard. That was strange since I had a recent oil change. I was fortunate that even though I was very naïve and did not go right to the gas station for more oil, somehow we made it all the way back to Framingham two days later without ceasing the engine.

Lisa's driving odyssey was a complete mystery to me, and as always with her, I was feeling completely in the dark. At this point all that was important was that Robert was safe with me again. One other piece to this mystery drive was the long scrape that was located on the passenger side of the front door that was about a foot up from the ground, which was about the same height as the sidewalk along the Bourne Bridge. I figured that she must have missed the exit to Mattapoisett and driven another 5 miles to the bridge, and in her drunken state must have for a moment scraped the car along the walkway. And because there was very little oil in the car, she must have left the car running when she pulled over to black out. This is all speculation, because I could never get the truth from her either because she was too embarrassed to tell me or that she just could not remember from her blacking out. I was frustrated again to not know the truth, but also that she would put our son in such a dangerous situation and not feel any remorse. It seemed any control I thought I had was slipping away.

PSYCH WARD ~

A few days later, while I was back at work, Grandma Leslie was down visiting our kids. I called to check in at 3:00 to make sure all was well. Lisa said that they were going to the grocery store to pick up some necessary staples. I told her not to go anywhere unless her mother was going to drive, because I knew that she would have been drinking. I then told her not to go until I got home and that I would arrive before 5:00. When I opened the front door to our house I was instantly confronted by Leslie. She said that they had gone to Stop & Shop, and that Lisa's driving was completely erratic and that I needed to do something right away.

"Why did you let her drive knowing that she was drunk?" I asked.

She did not answer and immediately put the blame on me! Lisa looked intoxicated with her silly grin and red face. She obviously had been drinking. I got on the phone and called her doctor to ask what should I do in this situation? He said get her to the hospital so that she can detox immediately, and that he would call Newton/Wellesley Hospital to arrange a bed for her.

I felt relieved that I had someone that knew what they were doing to protect my family. I told Lisa to pack her things and that we were going to the hospital. She was not pleased, but she complied. When we arrived there about an hour later, we had to wait a while to be "in-taked". So all the while Lisa kept asking to leave and saying that she did not need to be there. I stayed calm, and told her this was the best place for her now. She knew she was not going to change my mind. This was the best place for her to keep herself safe.

After the nurse had her all set up in her room, I drove home. I was relieved and hopeful that she would get detoxed and then be on the road to recovery. A while after being home the doctor called. I told him that she was now at Newton/Wellesley Hospital detoxing.

"So tell me, what are you most worried about?" he asked.

My next sentence would change everything, meaning I would lose any sense of control I thought I had.

"I am most worried that Lisa is drinking and driving," I said. "She drove down to Mattapoisett drunk with our son Robert, and now again today with the other kids in the car!"

"She has been driving drunk with your kids in the car?" he repeated. "I am going to file a 52A on her and have her committed to the psychological ward of the hospital."

I now felt panic once again and asked, "What does that mean?"

"It means that she is a danger to your family, as well as others," he said, "and that the Department of Social Services will be called in to evaluate her and the welfare of your family."

I said, "This will only anger Lisa! Is there anything else

we can do without calling in DSS?"

"No.," he replied. "It is state law. I have to contact them. It is for the good of your family."

I hung up the phone knowing that I was the cause of all the trouble that was coming. In one instance, I had brought the dreaded DSS into our home without even knowing that I had been heading down this dark and slippery slope. I felt that the one person that I could trust had turned on me. I was in great fear of learning from Lisa what they were going to do to her, and it was my fault. If I had just kept my mouth shut...but as I was saying this to myself, nothing added up. I found that I could not control this alcoholic, and yet I was supposed to know what to do at each crazy turn of this disease. I was in a no-win situation. My family was counting on me to know what to do, and I was failing at every juncture.

Soon after, I did receive a call from Lisa. She asked, "What are you doing to me? They have me locked down in a room in the psych ward. Why did you do this to me?"

"All I did was tell the truth to your doctor," I said. "What was I suppose to do? He asked me what I was most concerned about, so I told him. I did not think that all this was going to happen to you."

It started out that she had one too many drinks, and that she had gone to detox to get sober. Now it had turned into a much bigger problem for my family. The family secret was now officially out of the bag! I was feeling very guilty, now that she was angry at me, and trusted me even less. What had I done? In Lisa's mind she had done nothing more than have one too many drinks. In reality it was much more, and her doctor knew this. I was just trying to keep my family on an even keel and not bring attention to the problem. But now an entire agency and a hospital detox unit was into our lives. More and more of the camel's nose was poking into our tent, and there was now no way of pushing it away. I was in a panic, because I knew about those horror stories of DSS taking kids away from their own parents and placing them with foster families. Also, if Lisa was under investigation, so was I. I had nothing to hide, but the truth was that the kids were in danger while Lisa was alone with them. Lisa would now have to tell the truth about her drinking after hiding it from the world for so long. That was the only positive that I could take away from this situation.

DSS

A few days after Lisa had been released from the Newton Wellesley Hospital detox unit, we were contacted by an agent from the Framingham Department of Social Services. He wanted to set up a meeting at our house in the next couple of days. I did not discuss a strategy with Lisa, because I thought it was quite obvious what we needed to do. Tell the truth and say that we are both going to counseling for help in dealing with our family and the drinking problem, which in turn would get the agency out of our lives as soon as possible.

A few days later when I came home from work, I found an older gentleman sitting across the kitchen table from Lisa and her mother. He looked fairly expressionless when he shook my hand. I thought this was very strange that Leslie was attending this family meeting. She had nothing to do with this except for being a third, opinionated wheel in this conversation. The DSS agent then looked at me as if I were guilty of something, and said, "So I hear you have not been buckling up your son in the car seat?"

That was the very moment when I knew I had just been thrown under the bus so that Lisa could divert the attention away from herself. I was stunned and angry that Leslie was allowing the conversation to go this way. She knew that her daughter was drinking and driving, because she had been in the car with her to be an eye-witness to the whole ordeal. Now she was letting Lisa get away with this, and I was left trying to defend myself.

I told the agent that at times I had difficulty getting Andrew buckled into his seat because he fought me on it, and there were times that he would unbuckle himself while the car was in motion. I was not always able to pull over, because of the road not having any space to do so, but this rarely happened. I hoped my answer would suffice. I did not tell him that Lisa had been recently pulled over by the police because Andrew had unbuckled himself and stuck his head outside the window. I felt that this would just aggravate the agent and also steer him down a path that had nothing to do with her drinking. Leslie had ganged up on me, and instead of being the voice of reason she had pointed the enabling gun right at me! Lisa was no longer a person that I could trust, and neither was her mom.

I was now alone in my fight to reveal the truth and in danger in my own house. I had to completely change the way I looked at my marriage, and how I was now going to act around my wife. Lisa had done the unthinkable. She had thrown away her husband and the safety of her kids for the sake of drinking. By putting up a smoke screen she was able to keep the DSS agent from getting to the truth, and she had placed doubt in my corner as a decent father. I thought that putting Robert in danger by driving drunk to Mattapoisett would be enough to get this agency to give us help, but with Lisa avoiding the truth at all costs, help was a long way off.

A few days later the DSS agent had each of us go to his office separately so that he could find the real truth. I was slightly encouraged that he asked me to this meeting, so I could tell him my side. He still wanted to know if I was indeed driving around with Andrew and the other kids unbuckled. I told him absolutely not. He also told me that he had persisted in getting to the truth about Lisa's drinking and driving, and that she had reluctantly told him that she had a glass of wine before she had begun driving that day. I did not want to add anything more to her story fearing that they would have just cause in taking our kids away. He said that he would suspend the case if we continued to go for counseling. I told him that we would.

I had been going to a counselor in Newton thinking that he understood. The counselor in one of our sessions asked if it would be OK to contact the DSS agent to report in to let him know of our progress. I said that would be fine. Lisa had also been doing joint sessions with her counselor out of Wayland and mine, thinking that we could uncover the real reason for her drinking, and helping me to cope with an active alcoholic. But I finally gave up on these joint sessions as well as my own when my counselor made the recommendation that I should drink with Lisa to keep tabs on her! I think what he was trying to say that by my drinking with her that I might better understand her drinking, and possibly rebuild trust with her. Although he never said that, Lisa's counselor quickly stated that was not a good idea. I decided it was not a good idea to continue seeing this quack who apparently had no clue or credentials in advising anyone regarding alcoholism.

After a few weeks, he spoke to Lisa's counselor stating that if I did not make another appointment with him that he would call the DSS agent to let him know that I had broken the agreement. I was furious. He was blackmailing me, so that I would continue seeing him and paying for bad advice. I called my attorney the next day to let him know what was happening. He said that he would be glad to write a letter to get this guy off my back. After receiving this letter a week later, my counselor said that he would run this by his lawyer. In the end, he found that he had no leg to stand on, and I was rid of him.

During this time the DSS agent had left the agency in Framingham and the case was officially closed. I was relieved, but very cautious, because I knew if this case were opened again that there would be two strikes against us. The real problem was that Lisa was willing to throw me away, as well as our kids, so that she could keep drinking. At this point she was willing to sacrifice everything she had and the only person that truly stood in her way was me.

NO TIME TO CLEAN

The entire episode with the DSS agency was only a temporary fix. Even though outside eyes had been on her, Lisa had successfully fooled them and was free to go about her usual business. She seemed a little more cautious the way she went about her day, and I kept a very low profile because I did not want to rile her in any way. I knew that her wrath could get me in a lot of trouble. I did not trust anyone at this point, except my immediate family. I was concerned that we now had a file on us, and I was not going to have the chance to go through what the agent had written. If there were no further problems, then it would be a moot point, but if there were another incident, then I would need to have a copy for my records and possible for a day in court.

The big problem was that Lisa had made an entire agency believe that her drunken driving episode with a six-month-old in the back seat was a onetime occurrence, when the truth was just the opposite. But if I had said anything to contradict her, then I would have brought the agency down on her, and then she in turn would make me the bad guy accusing me of not telling the truth. Who was this biased agency going to believe? I knew all too well. I was going to do everything in my power to control Lisa, so that she would be unable to make any huge, wrong moves. I had no plan to make this long shot work, but I would figure something out.

While Lisa had been in the Newton Wellesley Hospital it gave me a few days to try and clean up all the piles of mess that had accumulated all over the house. Our family name could have been changed to "The Hoarders." There were piles of clothes, toys, and miscellaneous stuff that had been randomly bought over the past few years through EBay and local stores. Our bedroom was very messy, so I decided to start with Lisa's closet. I came across a clear bag full of letters, and notes that she had written. I only read a few pages, but it gave me great insight as to what trauma she had experienced. It gave me understanding as to why she drank. She had emotional trauma from her father, and knew only one way to cope with her guilt. I truly felt sad for her and worried that she was a walking time bomb of terrible secrets that were about to take down the lives of those she loved.

She was becoming more and more nervous that her true self was being questioned by strangers, as well as by her husband. She too ironically could trust no one, and if she did let anyone in, then she would lie her way through. While running around the house frantically picking up clothes, toys, and junk, I became aware that I was losing to the clock. Time was moving quickly that I knew Lisa would be home in just a few days, and I would not have enough time to clean up or cover up the mess that she had left behind. I also had three children to feed, bathe, and get to their activities, as well as put them to bed at a reasonable hour. Trying to fit in a week's worth of cleaning when there was almost no time to do it was a recipe for failure. All I could do was fold clothes as neatly as possible and put them into garbage bags, which I piled up in our old 1700 room to get them out of the way, but this would also allow Lisa to go through and see what she wanted to use. I knew when she came home that she would be on the attack mode knowing that her family secret was slowly slipping out and that there was nothing she could do about it but deny it ever happened. I could not ask her mother for any help because she was a pro at enabling and taking Lisa's side. I did not want that in my house again. I was trying to bring back sanity, but it was soon going to once again vanish.

TAKING INVENTORY

As soon as Lisa arrived back home a few days later, she immediately walked around the house and took inventory of what I had done. She took it as an assault that I had touched her personal belongings. I told her that all I had done was get things off the floor, and that I did not throw anything of hers away. I said that it had become difficult just to walk around our bedroom without tripping over discarded clothing.

She did not buy into my explanation and, in fact, began to take things out of the very bags that I had piled up, and to bring them back into our bedroom just to make a moral stand. I felt very guilty, but did not have an answer for her hoarding, and she would not offer me any solution to this problem. After reading her diary, I knew that all she felt was that I once again mentally abused her. I began to regret that I had ever spoken to the doctor or tried to help Lisa. All I was getting was a lot of flack that I did not deserve. Now that she was back in the house nothing was going to change, except that her distrust for me was ever increasing. I was in her way of both her drinking and her hoarding. I felt that this situation was not going to end in my favor, but I still had a speck of hope that something would give. And all this had happened even before the DSS agent had entered our house. I still felt like a sitting duck, because nothing had changed, and the DSS agent did not do anything that would help our family or get Lisa into the real treatment program that she needed. It was now just a matter of waiting for another crazy event.

POOL CLUB FIASCO

That summer of 2000 was more of the same. Lisa was hiding her drinking, and I was left wondering what I was supposed to do. I never knew what I was coming home to, but I lived in the world of denial that was going to keep me sane and my family safe. One afternoon in August, as president, I had set up a board meeting with the members on the Belknap Pool committee to meet at the pool club at 3:00. I told Lisa that I was going, and to only call the pool if she needed me for anything important, and that I would only be gone for about an hour.

A few minutes after I had arrived, I saw Lisa walking into the club with her friend Cindy. The only problem was that I had brought Andrew and Krista with me, but she had left Robert by himself at home! I knew this was going to be trouble, especially when Cindy saw that Robert was not with me. The only thing she would think was that Lisa had been totally irresponsible leaving her youngest unattended.

I asked Lisa where was Robert, and she just looked at me blankly. I told her to stay at the pool and that I was going home to get Robert. I flew home, and found Robert safe in his crib, but the damage was already done. I brought him back to the pool club, but I did not get a chance to talk to Cindy about what had happened and to try and make things right or in other words, to cover Lisa's tracks. I was not happy, and could only hope that Cindy would not tell anyone what she saw.

I could feel the calm before the storm, but felt nothing for about a week, and then it came back with a vengeance. During that time, I had spoken to our one-time alcohol therapist Meghan who had moved to Maine with her husband. She had left her number with us in case we ever needed to speak to her in an emergency. I called her and told her that Lisa's drinking was completely out of control, and that I needed help in placing her in a real treatment program. She told me to call The Brattleboro Inn located in Brattleboro Vermont, and they would hopefully have a room for her in which she could remain for a longer period of time than just a few days. She needed real therapy, and the staff there was some of the best.

I called and told them of my family's plight. They agreed that she needed real help, and that they would open a space for her as soon as a bed was available. I felt a surge of hope for the first time, thanks to Meghan. That afternoon Lisa received a phone call from her therapist in Wayland. All I heard was Lisa swearing and yelling at the person on the other end of the phone. This was not good. She yelled that she had no right to do this to her, and that her friends did not have the right to speak about her behind her back. I asked her what was going on, and she said that Cindy had told her other friend Angela that she had left Robert alone in the house while they went to the Belknap Pool, and that Angela had mentioned this to the therapist who she and Lisa both went to.

Lisa was incensed that one of her friends would talk about her behind her back without knowing the whole story. The therapist said that she, by law, was required to contact DSS to protect the children. I asked Lisa to hand me the phone so that I could speak to her. I got on the phone and said that Robert was left alone for less than 10 minutes and that he was safe, and that I had contacted The Brattleboro Inn to make arrangements for her to be admitted as soon as a bed was available. She said that she had no other recourse, and that she was going to call DSS. Lisa was so angry that she called Angela right after the phone call with the therapist and ripped her a new one. Angela knew the call was coming, because she had spoken to Cindy about the fact that after her session with the therapist she had been told what was going to happen next. They tried to find a way to lessen the blow for themselves, but there was no way of making this wrong right.

BRATTLEBORO INN

After Lisa had yelled at Angela, I decided to write a letter to her stating that under no circumstances was she allowed to speak to their therapist about Lisa. I felt it was truly an invasion of privacy and since she had not witnessed the incident, it gave her no right to speak from hearsay. I had Lisa sign the letter, and I mailed it the next day. I was frustrated because I had made contact with the people running the Brattleboro Inn in Vermont from the recommendation of our first therapist Meghan. They told me that as soon as they had a bed ready that they would call us. I had done everything I could up to this moment to get Lisa well, but outside forces thought they knew better. They just made matters worse, and I was left to once again clean up the mess.

 The call came about a week later. The woman at the Brattleboro Inn said they had a room available, but Lisa would have to be there the following day by noon or she would lose her bed. I was thrilled, but also knew that I would have to sell Lisa on the fact that she would be away from home for a while, but it was well worth the time away from her family. She reluctantly agreed, and so I called my parents to let them know what we were doing. I made arrangements to go to the Mount Mansfield Trout Club near Stowe Vermont for a few days with Andrew and Krista to have some fun swimming and boating and to gain some peace. Robert was too young to go with us, and my parents were very happy to take care of him for the weekend. I thought it might be easier on Lisa if the kids came to lessen the blow of abruptly saying good-by to them.

She had enough time to pack and get a good night's sleep, but also I feared time to talk herself out of going. The next morning after eating breakfast, it was time to leave. Lisa now began to have major second thoughts and was making excuses not to go. I stood fast and kept saying that she had no choice, and that it was the right thing to do for our family. I had called my parents to come over to pick up Robert and to give Lisa moral support and assurance that everything would be fine while she was gone.

It was almost 10 o'clock, and I thought time was running out. It would take almost two hours to get there, and I did not want to take any chances missing this one opportunity to hopefully kick her mind off of alcohol. Once my parents had arrived, I said, "It's time to go...Everybody in the car now!" Lisa made one final excuse to not go, but we helped her into the car, and closed the door behind her. The kids were very excited to go to Vermont and were happy that we were all together driving. On the way up to Vermont we did not say a whole lot. The drive was easy with very little traffic on a Saturday morning, and we made it 15 minutes before noon.

The staff at the facility was very nice and the campus was beautiful. We were able to go to her room after checking her in, but we were not allowed to stay too much longer so that she could get settled. We all gave her a big hug, and I told her how proud I was of her, but I could see that she was not happy to be there. When the doors to her floor closed I noticed that they were locked and that there was no way to get in or out. Lisa did not like being closed in or locked in, and I could only imagine what was going through her mind. I was very happy to be driving to a much-needed mini vacation, and I knew the kids would have a blast swimming and not having to worry about momma. To help ease Lisa's mind, I told her that we would stop by on the way back from the Trout Club. The weekend flew by swimming, boating, and eating great food, and we did not have a care in the world. But now it was time to drive the five hours back to Framingham with a very brief visit with Lisa.

The drive back to Brattleboro was about two hours. When we arrived, we asked to see Lisa. I was not sure if we were doing the right thing seeing her so soon, but I knew it meant a lot to Lisa and the kids. Upon seeing her, she appeared frustrated and annoyed. She focused on the fact that she had to ask to leave the floor, and that everything was regimented and controlled. She felt as though all her freedoms had been taken away. I told her that she needed to stay to let them do their job in getting her and keeping her sober. She did not ask to go home with us, which I was pleased about. We got to see her single room again now that she was acclimated to her new surroundings. But after a half an hour it was time to leave, to allow her the time to heal. We drove away, and now it was my time to be a full time parent without a wife to help. I was up to the challenge, and I was very excited to be able to be in charge without any crazy undermining from within and the outside world.

A few days later after arriving home, I received a phone call from Lisa. She said that one of the men in her group therapy sessions was coming on to her, and that she felt very uncomfortable being there. Of course I was very concerned, so after we spoke I made another phone call to the director of the facility. He assured me that if this were taking place that they would correct this problem immediately. I felt relieved but also wondered if this was not just a ploy on Lisa's part to get me to bring her home. Later I learned that this man was asked to leave, so Lisa was going to feel safe at the Inn and be able to focus on her substance abuse addiction.

HOME ALONE WITH MY KIDS

Now that I was alone with the kids, I had to rely on my family to help out with the day care duties, especially my mother. I did allow Lisa's mom to come down and take Krista for a weekend or two. Krista enjoyed the special time with her grandmother, and as long as nothing weird was to happen on her watch, I was ok with it. I came home as early as I could each day to make sure Andrew was doing his homework and to do the daily chores as well as make dinner. John and Lynne had us over a few times to help ease my stress of making dinner all the time. Krista was taking dance lessons, and that was fun watching her learn from the cute dance instructor. I was having fun cleaning up the house, and feeling that I was not on guard all the time. I now had time to get the house back in order and the Fed Ex truck stopped coming to our house to make unwanted deliveries.

I finally received the call that I was dreading from a DSS representative. She wanted to make an appointment to come by and interview me, as well as observe the household situation. I was leery of what this woman would be thinking, especially with this being the second time they were called in to protect my family. I made the appointment with her, and then called my mother to let her know so that she could be available to watch my kids. Also, I thought it would be a good idea to have this woman see that my kids were being cared for not only by me, but also my extended family. The day that she arrived, I greeted her along with my mother. I took her around the house and introduced her to my children. I then brought her in to the old room to speak privately with her. I told her that Lisa was at the Brattleboro Inn and that I was handling the household duties well while she was away.

She observed that the house was still very messy even though I had spent some time packing and cleaning. There was still a lot of stuff around the house that I think caused her alarm. She believed that we still needed help and that we needed their services. I tried to influence her decision as best I could. I did not want them back in our house, especially when Lisa was going to be back on the scene. I knew that if anything was going to go wrong it was because Lisa was feeling threatened and would manipulate whoever was closest to her. My mother even tried to put on her most convincing positive face, but that did not sway this woman in any way. DSS was coming back into our house, but not until Lisa was home again. I was hoping that she would be away for at least a few months, but if history were to repeat itself, she would be home sooner rather than later.

I drove up to Brattleboro Vermont a few weeks after she had been admitted, because the therapist said that it would be a good idea to meet with both of us to figure out our dynamics, and possibly give us some guidance. I was more than happy to see Lisa again, and I thought that she would be happy to see me. When I did arrive, I had time to walk around the campus, and relish in the beauty of autumn in Vermont. The leaves were nearing peak, and I just loved this time of year.

Change was in the air, and I was very happy to see how Lisa was doing. I was going to give any kind of support that I could. She came out of the facility to say hello. It was not the most exciting greeting that I had expected. It felt as though there was still a chasm between us. When we hugged there was not much emotion to be felt. I was now on guard, but I felt that I was still the supportive husband, and that she should be impressed that I was there encouraging her on. When we met with the therapist, I became emotional and teary. Lisa did not appear moved by my emotions. I felt very much alone and felt that I did not get much out of the session. In fact, I did not feel that there was any positive change in Lisa at all. While I was alone with her, I tried to get intimate with her by kissing her, but there was nothing to build on, so I let my feeling of amour deflate. I felt dejected.

We had lunch together, and she said that she had met some of the most amazing people and that she was working hard at getting better. She also said that while she was walking around town with some of the other patients that they all felt the pull of going into the local package store but refused the urge to do it. I told her that I was proud of what she was doing, and that she should stay as long as possible to get the most out of her treatment. I spent some time in her room looking at some of her artwork and writing that she had done. She told me that she was looking forward to coming home soon. Part of me was happy that we would be together again and the other part was apprehensive, knowing that she would not be spending enough time working on the true problem. Being molested as a child would take years of hard-nosed therapy sessions. While speaking to the therapist, none of this past trauma was discussed. I did not feel that she was anywhere near ready to come home.

I thought that this was going to be our family's last hope that Lisa would get well, but in my gut I knew she was just biding time until they thought she was ready to leave. She could hold out that long, but where was that going to leave us? It was time to go, and we embraced for a moment, but I tried at the same time to not give her too much reason to want to come home. I fully believed that she needed a lot more time to undo the hell she had been put through for so many years. It was going to take a long time and a lot of hand-holding from people who could give her the real support that she needed. I was not capable of doing this for her. I was just hoping that she was not going to fool herself or the staff into believing that she was fine to go home. She was not. Not by a long shot.

After saying good-by, it was now time to drive the scenic Route 2 back to Framingham. I was looking forward to being back with my kids, but also felt a little sad that Lisa and I were going to be a part for a while. I missed her being home, and being intimate with her, but I could wait as long as needed if it meant that she was going to be well and have it stick this time. Before ending my trip back, I decided my Honda Accord needed a car wash, so I pulled into a local one in Ashland. The only problem was that I did not put my car into "neutral", so by keeping it in "drive" I kept bumping into the car ahead of me. I was so dazed from all that I had been through and all the driving I had done in one day that I did not pay attention to what I was doing. Luckily no damage was done to the car in front, but the driver was not too thrilled and neither was the car wash attendant. I was glad to get home in one piece.

MORE QUESTIONS UNANSWERED

When I arrived home, I was greeted by my three kids and my mom. I told them that Lisa was doing well and that she was getting the care that she needed. I also said that I was not sure when she would be coming home, but it would not be too much longer. My children were fine about it, and all was calm in our house. More than three weeks had gone by since visiting her in Brattleboro, but she called one day and said that she was ready to come home, and that she was making arrangements to come back by bus. I was not very happy about this, and also I wanted to be the one taking her home so that I could ask more questions from the people who had been treating her. She said that was not necessary, because they gave her the name of a local agency by the name "Connections" that would provide the support she would need in aiding her in her recovery. I had never heard of this group, but it was located in the heart of downtown Framingham, so I thought it would be convenient for her. I still believed that the best place for her was somewhere far away from all the triggers that had affected any chance of her sobriety.

    A few days later she took the bus home, and was back with the family. The children were very happy to see their mom, and she was happy to be with them. We tried to get right back into our roles in parenting and husband and wife. I still felt very much in the dark as to what I was supposed to do, because I had had no final conversation with her therapists. It was all confidential, which I understood, but at the same time it did not help the family as to what we needed to do for her and for ourselves.

    Lisa resented the fact that I had been home alone to do whatever I wanted as far as cleaning and packing up discarded clothes and what I felt were useless items just cluttering the house. I tried very hard not to throw things away that were hers, because I did not want to trigger anger, which might set her drinking off again. I was amazed how our family was right back to where we had left off before she had gone to Vermont. Nothing seemed to change, except for the fact that she was sober, but for how long?

NOTHING CHANGED ~

On the one hand it was nice having Lisa home. I felt it took a lot of the pressure off me and my mom for having to make up for one parent's duties around the house. I could focus once again on my business and leave the cooking and daily chores to her. Lisa has always been a very good cook, although I did enjoy the times that John and Lynne invited us over for dinner. We had a lot of fun, and it helped ease any anxiety the kids might have been feeling. I never heard any of our children complain or say they missed mommy. I know they did, but they also knew she was now in a safe place.

But now she was home again. We felt like a family with something missing. It was as if we had no foundation of peace and that there was something looming over us all the time. We wanted to go about our daily business and be a normal family, but everything was soon to change. About a week after Lisa had been home, we received a telephone call from Sally Bellis, the new DSS representative who was assigned to our case number two. She made an appointment to come over and observe our family. I was not happy that another DSS person was infiltrating our home. I was hoping that she would see the truth, and I was naïve enough to think she would.

The first day she came into our house she seemed a little aloof, and I knew that was her way of trying to be objective as to what she saw. The three of us sat around the kitchen table to discuss her intention and her plan for our family. She picked up right away that Lisa was not happy that she was there. I believed she feared that she would be found out, and sent packing again. Sally said right away that she felt that the Family Services that DSS and SMOC (South Middlesex Opportunity Counsel) offered would solve our family's issues. I sat there thinking that this woman does not have a clue of what was

TENTACLES.. THE ENTANGLEMENT OF ALCOHOLISM

really going on with our family. I was not enthusiastic at all about what she was suggesting, because I knew that Lisa would once again fool anyone whom she feared could harm her or whom she could manipulate in believing her story and taking her side. I could not say anything against it, because I was not sure what the program was, but I knew in my heart it would never work. I really did not have a choice.

Sally left some literature about the program for us to read, and then said that she would be back again the following week. I kind of trusted her, because I thought that if she had been through these situations before that she would see right through anything that did not fit into the puzzle, and that maybe she could finally give some sound advice and steer our family into the right direction. The next week that she came to visit I had just brought in the mail to the kitchen where Lisa was sitting down. She asked for the mail and I said, "No. I will take care of it". I meant that whatever credit card bills or new offers that she would receive that I would not allow her to get into any more trouble. What I did not realize was that Sally saw it as abusive and controlling on my part. I thought that she would understand what I was trying to do, but instead I could see the change of her expression and attitude towards me. And at that moment I could see Lisa had found that crack in the armor of getting on Sally's good side and getting her to take Lisa's side. At that point I knew I was in trouble.

From then on Sally aimed much of her attention to Lisa. She even took out her family photos and made a point to show Lisa, but not to me. I felt that I was on the hot seat and was being victimized for trying to stabilize a crazy situation, but now I had an entire agency led by an ignorant woman out to get me. My family was in terrible trouble, and Lisa was off the hook and in charge of the asylum. Sally Bellis was going to do everything she could to bring justice to this poor woman who had been wronged without knowing all the facts of what really had been going on for years. Somehow I had to convince her otherwise, but I did not have a plan. I had to just play defense until some miracle was going to change her mind.

BROWN PAPER BAG

A few weeks after our first meeting with Sally Bellis, I found what I thought to be the miracle that I was looking for—the miracle that would convince her and the agency that Lisa did indeed have a drinking problem. I found a brown paper bag with empty small wine bottles and a receipt from Kappy's Liquours hidden under the couch in our old room. I quickly brought it upstairs into my office and called Sally to let her know what I found, and that I would like a meeting with her the next day. She agreed. I let Lisa know that she was coming over tomorrow just to make sure she would be available to take part in the meeting. What I did not realize was the craftiness in Lisa's thinking. She knew right away something was up. When I went back to my home office the next morning just hours before the meeting was to be held, the bag of bottles, and my only evidence was gone from where I had placed it behind my office door. Lisa had gone back to where she had stashed her loot. When she found that it was gone she had to find it to protect her façade. I was in a panic, because in just a few hours I would have nothing to show, and then it would look awfully fishy that I was trying to manipulate an agency in believing something that I had no proof. My heart sank, because I knew that Sally would have more ammunition into making the case that I was a terribly abusive husband.

Sally arrived at 10 o'clock with one of her associates named Sally also. Lisa was upstairs taking a long bath. It was just me and the two Sallys sitting across from me at the kitchen table not saying very much. When Lisa did finally come into the kitchen 20 minutes later she looked very red in the face and disheveled. The four of us sat at the kitchen table, and Sally asked me why I needed an unscheduled meeting. I told her what I had found, but today when I went to retrieve the bag it was gone. Lisa turned to Sally and said in a shaky quivering voice, "Sally, I would never lie to you. If I had a problem with drinking, I would tell you".

I immediately said, "No! That is untrue! I did find a bag of wine bottles! Why else would I have called you?!"

I also pounded the table with my fist once to drive home my point. Sally was not impressed, nor did she believe me. She said that she and I should go into the next room to discuss this further. She said, "I noticed that Lisa did not come downstairs for a while when I got here. That seemed strange to me. Why don't you go to work, and I will take care of this and talk to Lisa further".

I thought, maybe she was getting it after all. I went to work leaving the two of them back at our house as hopeful as I could be under the circumstances. Maybe now there would be a new plan in place to focus on Lisa's drinking problem.

SALLY'S DECISION ~

When I arrived at work I had plenty to keep me busy. I was hoping that Sally would have a real heart to heart with Lisa, and that maybe something would get resolved. At 2:30 my phone rang in my office. It was Sally. She said, "After speaking to Lisa, we thought it would be a good idea for her to go to her mother's and take the kids with her."

I was stunned. This made no sense to me, especially since she was still actively drinking! I told her that this was a terrible idea, and that it was placing my kids in danger.

"No matter," she said. "We see no evidence that she has been drinking, and it would be better to take the kids out of this situation."

After hanging up the phone, I went to my Managing Partner's office to let him know what was happening and to get some much needed advice. He was shocked at what DSS had proposed, especially when there were two cases of neglect open on Lisa. He told me to get home right away to see what was really going on, and maybe make some sense of all this. I took off from Wellesley, and made it home within 20 minutes. When I walked into the house I found, to my relief, that both Sallys were not there. I wanted to talk sense into Lisa to explain to her that this was a nutty idea to take the kids to her mother's apartment. Where would the kids sleep, and more importantly she was in no condition to drive anywhere. She just replied in an emotionless tone, "This is what Sally wants us to do."

I was in a panic. I did not want her taking the kids anywhere, especially all the way to Lunenberg an hour away. I called up the DSS agency and asked for Sally.

"Is there anything else we can do to avoid Lisa taking the kids out of our house?" I asked.

She replied, "Not that I can think of."

Even though I did not want to make this suggestion, I did not see any other way. I said, "What if I leave the house, and go to my parents' house for the night, so this way my kids won't have to be interrupted from their daily routine?"

There was a brief silence over the phone, but then she replied, "I guess that will be fine."

The last thing I wanted to do was leave my own house in the hands of a drunk. But without Lisa's cooperation, and her ability to think rationally, I thought this was the only alternative to placing my kids and the other drivers on Route 495 in serious danger. So I told Lisa what I was planning on doing, and she was fine with it.

I called my mother to tell her what was happening, and that I would be over before supper. I could tell by the sound of her voice that she was very concerned that I was leaving the kids with Lisa in her state of mind and inebriated condition. I stalled as long as I could by getting my clothes and business files together to be able to go to work the next day. I also had an appointment to go to after dinner that I had to prepare for. After giving the kids a big hug, and explaining to them that I had to leave for the night, I drove the mile to my parent's home.

AT MY PARENTS' HOUSE

When I arrived at my parents' house, I told my mother that this was it—that I could not take it anymore. I then called my brother John and told him that I had decided to divorce Lisa, because of what she had done. He did not say much, but I knew he felt relief that I was finally taking the right course of action to protect my kids. Soon after, I called Luke Penny, the son of my father's estate planning attorney, who was a client of mine. He specialized in difficult divorce cases. When I got him on the phone, I told him exactly what was going on with my wife and the DSS agency. He told me that I should sit tight and not to go near our marital home, because I would probably be arrested. He said that he wanted to call the DSS agency to find out exactly what was going on. I gave him my consent.

About 15 minutes later he called back. The first words out his mouth were, "You're fucked. They believe that there is more going on between you and your wife than has been portrayed. In other words they think you are abusive to your wife. I told them that you had volunteered to leave the house to keep your kids safe. Ms. Bellis could not understand why you did this."

I told him the reason that I did. He understood, but they were actually using this selfless action against me! I then asked him what should I do?

"You will need to meet at my office tomorrow morning," Luke said. "We are going to file a vacate order to remove your wife out of the house. But to do this you will have to write up a summation of what has transpired these past few years, as well as get two people you know and trust that can corroborate your story."

I called up Cynthia, my assistant of 5 years, to ask her if she would be willing testify if needed. She said that she had witnessed Lisa trying to hold baby Robert while intoxicated when she and her husband had stopped by our house one day. She said that she was very concerned at what she saw. In fact, she and her husband remained in the driveway until I came home 30 minutes later. I was relieved that she had the courage to help me and my family out. The only other person that I felt I could call was Lisa's friend Cindy who worked at the Framingham Day Care Centre just down the road. It was she who had also witnessed Lisa's leaving Robert home alone when she went to the Pool Club. I thought surely she would want to help keep my kids safe. I would drive down to where she worked the following morning and ask her for her testimony.

In the meantime, I had to write my report, which I would do in the morning. I thought it was a good idea to keep my appointment with my clients in Cambridge, so that this way I could keep my mind from going too crazy about my situation. A few months earlier I was speaking to another client who had recently lost his wife to ovarian cancer. He had asked her before she died how would he know when she was around him? She simply said, "Look for the penny." He told me that since then whenever he is in a stressful situation, a penny appears in the strangest places and gives him comfort. That night when I was walking from my car to my client's house, there in the middle of the street was a shiny penny! I started to laugh to myself. It was at that moment I knew everything was going to turn out all right.

INSTANT RECALL ∾

The next morning I woke up early before 5:00 so that I could write up my report to give to my attorney. I was able to recall all the craziness that I had witnessed and been a party to. I wrote for two hours and completed 10 pages of alcohol history. My next move was to drive down to the Framingham Day Care Centre and speak to Cindy. I walked into the main office where I found Cindy sitting and asked if I could have a word with her. She agreed, and so we went into one of the classrooms so that we could have some privacy. I had told her what had happened, and that I needed her help. She listened quietly, and then told me she really did not want to say or do anything that would hurt her relationship with Lisa. I tried to reason with her that without her testimony my kids would remain in danger, and that our family really needed her help. She politely refused, and I was dumbfounded. She had witnessed terrible parenting and told Angela all about it, and then did not have the courage to tell the truth.

I walked away in disbelief. I called my attorney and told him I had only one person who would testify on our behalf. He said that would be fine and to meet him in his office in one hour. When I arrived I did not feel right. This whole thing was going too fast. My mind was not ready to take such legal action, one that would greatly affect my kids, my wife, and my life. As Luke spoke and went through the process of going before a judge, and what we were going to say and do, he could tell through my eyes that I was not ready. He stopped in mid sentence.

"You aren't ready for this are you?" he said.

"No, because it just doesn't feel right," I said. "I need more time to figure this out and get my brain wrapped around this."

He understood and knew that if I was not ready, then it was not the right time to move forward on the divorce. I told him I really appreciated all his advice, and that I would pay him for his time. Then I drove back home to my house where I was not sure what kind of reception I would receive. I drove into our driveway to find Leslie's car parked there. When I walked into the house I found both Lisa and Leslie sitting in the kitchen acting like nothing out of the ordinary had taken place. This was very weird. Lisa had called her mother down to help take care of the kids, but she was not at all angry or had any negative feelings towards me whatsoever. I was glad that I was allowed in the house. My attorney had told me that I would probably be arrested if I tried to get back in. On the contrary, it was if this moment in time had never taken place. This was the first time I had left my house, and it made me feel almost like I was a stranger in my own world. Leslie stayed for a while and then decided to leave, because there was no reason now for her to be there. I was happy to see her go. I told Lisa I had been at my attorney's office to try and decide what to do about our situation. She did not seem all that alarmed by my admission. In her mind, there was no problem, as long as she could continue doing what she was doing. I felt trapped in her drama, and once again was a prisoner in her disease.

IMMUNE ~

After coming back into the house, one thing I did realize was that Lisa and her mother's nonchalant reaction to what had just transpired was the fact that this craziness was what they had experienced for years with Dan Sr. They were so immune to such inappropriate behavior that they had learned to react and then shut off from the truth. It was their way to cope. I did not understand, but at the same time I did.

The terrible thing was that this was acceptable behavior, and I had to go along for the ride or decide not to, but either way I was going to have to make a decision for the safety and future of my children. I did not want them growing up thinking that crazy alcoholic behavior was the norm. I also became quite aware that I would have to change my behavior around Sally Bellis, because she had chosen her side. She was going to do everything in her power to protect Lisa, and in her eyes, protect the kids from me, because I was the cause of our family's problems. I decided to give her no emotional power over me. If I was going to survive, I was going to have to keep myself in check at all times.

There was no one in my house that was going to protect me, except myself. And the bigger picture in all of this was the safety of my children. They were in danger, because Lisa's drinking had gotten so out of hand that whether she was at home or behind the wheel of our minivan she could not be trusted anymore. I was trying to single-handedly hold together a dam that kept having new leaks. I knew I could not do this by myself forever. I also knew that to end my misery was to use the only escape clause, and that was through my attorney. I just was not ready emotionally.

ROBERT'S WOUND

One night when I came home from work, I went to pick up Robert from his crib and found that he had a big gash on the back of his neck. It looked awful. I asked Leslie who had come down again for the day what had happened. She said that Lisa had tripped over boxes that I left in the hallway while she was holding Robert and dropped him. I was furious! How could Leslie allow Lisa to hold Robert while she was drunk?

This was the last straw for me. I needed to get Robert to the hospital to take care of this wound, but my hands were tied because the nurses would ask questions as to what happened to our baby, and I knew that it was very possible that they would take him as well as the other kids away from us.

I waited for Leslie to leave and until Lisa was in our bedroom taking a nap. Then I called my mother to tell her what had occurred. She said she would come down to check on Robert. When she arrived I showed her his neck. The wound did not require stitches, so we were able to patch him up properly. I still considered taking Robert to the hospital just so they would have a record of this event. But Lisa was due to get up to go to her Connections meeting, and I did not want to create a scene before she went. Then she would have more negative things to tell them about me.

I heard Lisa walking around our bedroom, so I knew she was getting ready to leave for her meeting. I told my mother it was ok for her to go, but we had to be more diligent in protecting little Robert from his own mother and grandmother. The wheels were really coming off the denial wagon, and I did not know how much longer I could circle the wagons around my family from the outside world. It was just a matter of time.

BEN FRANKLIN APPROACH

One day I arrived at a client's office 20 minutes early, so I thought I would try to figure what I should do about my situation with Lisa by doing the Ben Franklin approach to making the right decision. I took a piece of white paper and wrote "Pros" on the top left side and "Cons" on the top right, and drew a line down the middle of the page. Then I began to write the reasons to stay with Lisa on the left hand side, and all the negatives on the right. I figured that would give me some concrete proper perspective on our living situation. The most important Pro was the fact that she was the mother to our children. Another was that she was an excellent cook and kept our family fed very well.

But then I began to write all the negatives, which began with words like "endangerment", "lying", "stealing", "driving drunk", and "manipulation", and "lack of love". The right side of the page was full, but the left hand side was only about a quarter of the way down the page. This opened my eyes as to just how dire and unhappy my life was with this woman. It felt cathartic to have written these words. I was not about to take any action at this time, but it did help to get a reality check. I stuffed the page into my briefcase and went into my meeting forgetting all about what I had written.

POLE NUMBER 29

I glance at the bottle on the floor
But I'm driving too fast to make the score
My eyes are fixed on the label
A fine year to put on the table
Longing for you like a lover
One more taste and I won't recover
More more more
I know I'm your favorite whore
Reaching for you it can't last
Looking up I see broken glass
I've just hit pole number 29
Damn that wine!
Failing the breathalyzer test
It's time for an arrest
I blame you for everything
But reality hurts like a bee sting
Pole number 29
I can no longer walk a straight line

    Lisa had made friends with an old acquaintance of mine from the Unitarian church we belonged to. Rebecca was a woman with whom I had grown up, and she became a successful entrepreneur opening two Children's Orchards clothing stores in Natick and Framingham. She liked Lisa and offered her a job running the Natick store. I was thrilled because it would give her something to do outside the house and hopefully would keep her mind off of her need to drink.
    Lisa began to work a few days a week to get her feet wet back into the working world. She liked it right away, and I thought maybe this would help keep her out of trouble. I also thought that maybe she could use her income to help repay

her Ebay habit that had proved quite costly to me. Rebecca did not know about Lisa's drinking problem, and I did not think it was my place to tell her, because maybe this was going to be her new start. I did not want to jeopardize her having this opportunity to be successful or to have another person know about her problem.

One Saturday morning while I was in the upstairs guest bathroom cleaning out the small closet behind the sink, my son Andrew came up to me and said, "Dad, look what I found in Mommy's purse?" He showed me a little nip bottle that she had hidden. I was disturbed that he had felt like he needed to go through her purse, and also upset that she was still drinking. He asked me what I should do about it. I told him there was nothing I could do, but if he wanted to tell his mother what he had found that was up to him. I felt that if he brought it up to her that would force her to tell him the truth.

A little while later he came back up stairs to tell me that she had said that she had found the bottle and was getting rid of it. I was very sad but not surprised that she could not even come clean to our little boy. I was a little worried as to what she might do next, but I felt all I could do was remain silent and not let on that I knew she was still drinking. Either way she would lie to me, and I would receive no help from Sally Bellis. I felt that my "Higher Power" would take care of things, because this was far too crazy for me to handle. Lisa did not let on that Andrew had found anything and did not appear angry that he had been snooping. I did not want her paranoia to spill over onto him in some negative way.

I told her to take my Honda Accord, because we probably would go out and use the minivan later. She drove off to work before nine o'clock, and I was left alone with the kids for the rest of the day. We had a nice time and all was calm. I had called her at work earlier in the afternoon, and all sounded fine in her voice. Lisa was due home around five o'clock, but when the time was after six, I began to get a little anxious. I thought maybe she was just working a little later. I decided I should make dinner for the kids and not have the kids feel there was anything amiss. I received a phone call from her at seven o'clock. She was calling from the police station, and that she had been arrested. She said that she had been in an accident and totaled the car, and that she was very reluctant in calling me, because of the way I would react. I tried to react to her as calmly as I could, but I was pissed. I told her I would be down to the station as soon as I could find someone to look after the children. My parents were not home, so I called Lynne. I told her that Lisa had been in an accident, and that she had been arrested. She said that she and John would be right over. They arrived 15 minutes later and were wonderful. They did not let on the way they were feeling about Lisa. I knew though that this was going to be the catalyst for taking action towards her drinking problem once and for all.

POLICE STATION

I drove to the police station located in the heart of downtown Framingham and arrived by 7:30. As I entered the station, I saw Lisa sitting on a bench in the main entrance area. She did not say anything, nor did I. I then asked her if she was ok, and she said she was fine just a little shaken. But other than that, it appeared as if nothing had happened. A police officer appeared from the next room who turned out to be a friend of mine from our hockey playing days. He was very nice and supportive and did not react in a negative way to her at all. The officer said that Lisa would have to appear in the Framingham court on Monday, and that a court appointed attorney would represent her.

A few minutes later we were in the minivan driving home. It was all very surreal to me. She had totaled my car, and it felt once again there were no consequences to her actions. In a way I had wished that she had remained in jail at least overnight, so that she could have some repercussion to her drinking and driving drunk. When we arrived home, Lynne came around the corner from the kitchen. I thanked her for coming over and looking after our kids, and Lisa thanked her enthusiastically without a trace of embarrassment. Lynne handed me a slip of paper with a lawyer's name on it, and whispered, "Call him soon."

I just nodded. I was overwhelmed with the idea that my wife had just been arrested, and was going to court to find out what fate was in store for her. I felt helpless. I was glad that she had not been hurt or killed anyone heading in the opposite way. Lisa told me that she had stopped at a package store on the way home and bought some wine. She was already tipsy from her nip bottle that she had internally disposed of, and was reaching down to pick up the paper bag that contained the wine bottle. As she looked up, she saw that she had veered into the center of Grove Street with a car heading straight for her. She swerved, and drove headlong into a telephone pole. She had been going approximately 40 miles per hour and cut the pole in half with the sudden impact of the car. She said she remembers the air bags deploying, but that was all. She said the police officer that arrived was angry towards her and asked if she would blow into the breath analyzer to check her blood alcohol level. Her levels were well over the legal limit, and she was arrested on the spot.

I did not know what to say to her or the kids, so I just tried to hold it together and not say too much that might antagonize the situation. I went up stairs and typed an email to our minister to let her know that Lisa had been arrested for Driving under the Influence. Her emailed response was one word..."Hallelujah!" I knew she was very relieved for our family. What I did not realize was that the arresting police officer had written up a report and sent it to DSS into the hands of Sally Bellis. The following day she called, and said that she would like to come over and speak to us. I had no idea how she would treat Lisa or me. But I would be ready for whatever she was going to say.

IN COURT ∼

I was hoping that Sally Bellis would finally see the truth to our situation, and that maybe now she would come up with a rational solution to helping Lisa deal with her alcohol addiction. Or would she somehow blame me for Lisa hitting a telephone pole going 40 mph even though I was not even in the car? Since DSS received the report directly from the police department, even Sally could not distort what was fact. I finally had the truth on my side, and all I had to do was remain silent when she arrived in our house. In the meantime Lisa and I discussed what she was going to do about legal representation the next day. She said that she did not want any special treatment, and that she would use the court appointed attorney to represent her. I said that was probably not a good idea, because she would have a better chance at getting a lighter sentence with a qualified substance abuse attorney. She still said no, so I just let the whole conversation end at that.

That night in bed we did not say very much lying next to each other, so we just went to sleep. I was hoping that the next day in court would go fairly for her, whatever that meant. We arrived in the Framingham District Court at 9 a.m. after leaving off Robert at day care. I took the day off so that I could be with Lisa to support her, but she asked me not to hang around, and that I should come back after she called.

I guess she was feeling both embarrassed, and angry all at the same time. All I was going to end up doing was to antagonize her. I decided to drive to Robert's day care, so that I could tell the staff what was happening and to request an extra day a week to keep him safe. I got very emotional when I spoke to the director. She had no idea what had been going on in our family. But in the end they just did not have any additional hours to give us, so that meant I would have to rely on my mother to spend more time with him.

At noon I received the call from Lisa to come back to the court house to pick her up. When I did she told me that the judge had ordered that she lose her license for 90 days and that she must attend a mandatory weekly alcohol meeting located in the SMOC building near downtown Framingham. I was not pleased with the outcome of the sentence, because it meant that Lisa would be stuck alone at home all day without a car and nowhere to go. This was a recipe for disaster. What else was she going to do except find a way to drink to alleviate her anger and resentment towards me and her life?

What the judge should have done was order her to go away to get some real treatment for her alcohol abuse, but this time for a much longer period of time than what she received at the Brattleboro Inn. Unfortunately, this was the court's way of taking care of just another person's addiction problem with no real thought or reason. It was the quick and easy way out, and the least costly to the system. In the end their justice was doomed to failure.

ARREST REPORT ~

The next day Sally Bellis showed up at our house at 9 a.m. and showed very little emotion. She was all business and was now focused on Lisa's drunk driving arrest report. She still paid little attention to me, but at least now she had a report that backed me up as to the truth I had been telling her all along. We once again sat across from each other at the kitchen table. Lisa did not say very much. She just listened to what Sally had to say. Sally reviewed with us what was in the police report. She did not scold Lisa, but she did say that there was a new regimen that she would have to follow. She went over 10 requirements that Lisa had to comply with. I could feel my eyes rolling back into my head. This was never going to work. How could she follow a set of rules that only a rational person could follow? I did not say this to Sally, but my mind was screaming at her. This, just as the court's decision was going to end up in abject failure. It was the easy sane way to deal with a good person gone wrong. The practical common sense way to approach this was for the system to admit that Lisa was a sick alcoholic who needed hours of treatment, instead of allowing a very sick person to heal thy self. I did not say anything, because I knew she would not listen to me any way. The truth-teller was told early on to keep his mouth shut while the experts handled this situation.

Sally also said that it was time for Family Services to intervene to give us additional help that our family so badly needed. All I could think of was that I would once again have to prove my side of the story and would these new people get it? But for now, the eyes of DSS were off of me and totally on Lisa. I felt a little sense of relief, but I knew I was still on the firing line, because I was still living with an angry and defensive alcoholic. Sally left our house feeling like she had accomplished what she had set out to do, and at the same time, without ever losing face that maybe she had been completely wrong all along.

90 DAYS

Lisa's day in court took her off the road for 90 days. I was relieved that no other driver was in danger at this time. Part of me felt badly that she had been arrested, but my more sensible side was jumping for joy. I felt that I had a modicum of control back that I had lost for some time. Now I was back in the driver's seat. I was also torn about what to do about getting Lisa to her weekly meeting. It was an hour walk to SMOC, or she could ride a bicycle, or take a cab. I decided to drive her for the simple fact that I knew she would get to her meeting if she were in the car with me. I also knew that if she weren't in the car with me, she would continue drinking, and would never make it there. I have heard from others that they had done the opposite without any positive results, so I did what I thought was my least enabling best.

Lisa was not happy about attending a mandatory meeting, especially with me driving her. She did not say much during the drive over and did not tell me anything about the meeting when she was through. I felt disappointed that what I had thought was going to be a negative outcome was coming true. The court also assigned Lisa a probation officer to whom she had report to each week to make sure that she was following the court's rules. I was never allowed in on these meetings. In fact I was ignored completely. Once again I felt very much out of the loop. I was glad that Lisa was held accountable, but not happy that I could not be part of the discussions. I felt as though there was this openly secret meeting going on right in front of me—shades of Sally Bellis all over again. So I decided to go about my daddy duties, and just stay out of the way.

CALL THE COPS ~

I was in the middle of planning my annual GreenUp Day town-wide clean up event. I was in charge of organizing hundreds of volunteers to clean up trash throughout the town of Framingham, as well as the celebration right after the clean up ended at noon. I did not have a lot of time to worry about what was happening with Lisa. I was hoping that SMOC and the probation officer could handle her situation. The fourth annual cleanup effort went off without a hitch. It got great local news coverage, and we were able to clean up a ton of refuse from all points of the town. I was feeling awfully good about what I had accomplished with these wonderful volunteers. But I had noticed that Lisa was giving me the cold shoulder, and was not saying much to me. I figured that it was just the fact that she was being scrutinized and held accountable so not to be drinking. I knew she resented me, because I was not the one who had a sobriety problem. In her mind I was to blame for her drinking, and she would do whatever she could to prove it.

On the Saturday night of our church's annual spring dinner and fundraiser, I wished that I could attend. I knew my parents and my brother John would be going. It was always a fun night, but I had my hands full at home, so I decided not to go. Leslie had driven down from Lunenberg, and was giving me an attitude that I felt when we sat down for dinner. She was saying some nasty things about me, and no one was coming to my defense. I decided to remove myself from this nutty situation and go upstairs to clean the main bathroom. I thought that being away from Leslie and Lisa would help diffuse the rising negative feelings that were permeating throughout the house. As I had my head buried by the toilet, Andrew came running into the bathroom.

"Gramma and mom are saying some really bad things about you!" he said.

I lifted my head up from under the toilet and said, "Don't worry. As soon as she is gone things will calm down around here."

Lisa had snuck behind Andrew on the stairway to listen in on what we were saying to each other. I heard a sound from outside the door of the bathroom, so I checked out who was there. Lisa immediately turned around crying as she quickly moved down to the first floor. I was very confused as to why she was so upset, so I went down to ask what was going on. She shouted, "I heard what you said! I am going to take the children out of here!"

I began to panic not knowing what to do next. I had to protect my children from this crazy woman. And there was no way I was going to let Leslie be the get-away driver in this moment of insanity. While Lisa was in the kitchen with her mother, I called my brother John from my office on the second floor to tell him something terrible was about to happen here, and that I needed him to come over right away. He said that he would be right there. I watched him walk to the front door in a very matter of fact manner. I knew he was getting ready for a fight. I then gathered Andrew, Krista, and Robert and headed for the basement with him. I knew there was a phone down there where I knew I would probably have to call the police. Lisa poked her head from the landing of the stairway into the basement.

"I read what you wrote about me you son of a bitch," she yelled. "I am taking the kids with me now!"

"No you're not, and I am calling the police." I said, as calmly as I could.

I dialed 911, and the dispatcher answered and asked, "What is your emergency?"

"My wife is trying to steal my kids out of the house, and she's drunk!" I said.

The dispatcher said that they would send over a cruiser.

Lisa heard every word, and muttered "You bastard" as she turned around and went back to her mother.

John and I took the kids into the music studio part of the basement to try to think of our next move and to try and remain calm as best we could. A few moments later Leslie came walking in. I told John to stay between us. She tried her best to convince the children to follow her out of the room. I held Robert close to me while the other two defiantly said no to her. I was very pleased the way they stood up to this instigator. In their youthful eyes they knew what was going on and did not want to leave the house.

Leslie knew there was nothing she could do, especially with John as a witness to her actions, so she walked out of the basement. I knew the police would be arriving very soon, so I told John that I would go out the bulkhead and meet them in the front of the house. I told John that I hoped that they would not be arresting me tonight. I knew what kind of risk that I was taking. John told me just to remain calm when the police arrived, and to just explain what was happening. I walked to the front of the house by the driveway and saw two cruisers pulling up to our house. I walked towards them. As they came up to me I explained that my wife was drunk and that she wanted to take my kids with her mother to Lunenberg, and that she was in no condition to do this. The officer said that he would go into the house and talk to my wife, and the other would remain with me. I was surprised that the discussion between the police officer and Lisa only took a few minutes. The officer came back outside, and said that she had decided not to take the kids out of the house. He also said that he had been the arresting officer when he arrested her for DUI! He said that she had lied to him about drinking and driving. I was very much relieved. He said that if they had to come back again tonight that they would arrest me. I was not very happy about that! I asked if it was ok for my brother to stay with us for a while until things cooled down and until Lisa sobered up. The officer said that would be fine.

I went back into the basement through the bulkhead to check in with John and the kids. They were fine. Both Lisa and Leslie had stayed in the kitchen. They did not try again to take the kids. I asked John if he would be able to stay with us for a little while. He said he would, but had to let Lynne know, so that he could meet her later on at the church dinner. Leslie decided that she would leave, because there was nothing more that she could do to conspire with her daughter. As she was getting into her car, my parents drove up to our house and parked right behind her. They were heading to the dinner party and were just checking in. I let them know what had just transpired, and they were relieved that all was ok. I told them that they needed to leave so that Leslie could too. After Leslie had driven away, John and I and the kids went into the living room and closed all the doors so to keep crazy out.

Lisa opened the door and exclaimed, "Isn't this a wonderful family gathering!" We all at once started talking at her to justify why we had taken refuge together. She left the room in a huff, and went upstairs to bed. Apparently what had set her off was that while I was out with the kids, she snooped around in my office upstairs, and while going through my open briefcase found the Benjamin Franklin outline that I had written and forgotten about. She also showed Sally Bellis to throw more fuel onto the fire. I had no way of knowing that she had gone through my stuff, because I did not feel I had anything to hide. I was not going to go forward with any kind of legal action, but how was she to know? She already was paranoid and very much on edge knowing that she was under court-ordered scrutiny; the page she read just pushed her over the edge.

I was glad that John stayed over for another hour just to make sure that she would not come back down and cause a scene—one that would get me arrested. At this point I was not sure what she was capable of doing. John finally went off to the church dinner. I was very appreciative that he came through for me and my family. After I put all the kids to bed around nine o'clock, I was in the kitchen having a late snack when Lisa came into the room. She had sobered up enough to wake up, and she sheepishly said, "I am sorry for the way I acted".

I simply said, "Its' ok, but I don't know why you had to over react as you did? Let's talk again in the morning."

She left the room, and went back to bed. I, at that moment, took off my wedding ring and knew that all that had happened up to this time had indeed killed our marriage. My finger felt naked, but I felt justified in taking the symbol of our marriage off for the last time. I was not ready to leave her, but the time was getting closer. I soon went to bed and lay next to her. I felt very much alone and very much on my own.

AFTERMATH

When I woke up the next morning I had many thoughts going through my mind. Part of me felt relieved that there was still a soul with some empathy left inside my wife, but it really did not change the future outcome of our life together. I could not possibly live with this woman who created such chaos for me and my children. Intellectually I knew this to be true, but emotionally I was not ready to give up just yet. I still loved her, and that proved to be problematic for the decisions I would have to eventually make. Her saying that she was basically sorry for what she had done gave me a reprieve or an excuse to not move forward with any hasty decision that could possibly make things worse than they were now, although I could not fathom how this situation could get any worse. My only decision was based on keeping my kids safe from an inside terrorist. Lisa was a very ill woman, and I had to remain strong and in control to see us all move forward in a healthy way without losing everything that I had worked for. I also had to make sure that I kept my emotions in check, for if I lost it, then I could be arrested even though she was a pro at pushing my buttons. It did not matter. Once I crossed the line she would have control of our children, and that was a risk that I could not take. Even when I removed myself from the danger zone I was not safe, because she was so paranoid. I needed to be omnipresent. I had to be on top of her drinking, knowing when and where she was doing it, while at the same time trying to work and keep a house together. It proved just too much. I would have to let natural consequences take their natural course and pray that my kids would come out unscathed.

Fortunately, Lisa had made two very big mistakes in hitting a telephone pole and pissing off a police officer. If more and more people knew what was truly happening, maybe I was safer than I thought. I hoped that strike three would finally get me off the hook from all this and give me a much needed break.

Then I received a phone call from Lisa's brother Danny. He sounded very upset. Leslie had gone home and told him her distorted view what had gone on that night with the police arriving and their attempt to kidnap the kids from me. I told him in a very matter of fact tone that his sister had been arrested for DUI and that she was indeed an alcoholic. He was shocked that his baby sister had turned out just like him. She, like her brother, could not hold down a job, keep a long term relationship, or be a responsible person. Leslie had tried to put the blame on me, but I would have none of it. I told him the way it was, and he would have to assimilate all this into his rose-colored world.

Our phone conversation only lasted a few minutes, but it got the point across that he was part of an amazingly dysfunctional family where even the rock had major flaws. Lisa was now off the pedestal, and their family would eventually start to get well or be cast adrift. I knew the answer, and I was disgusted by how weak they all were.

I was expecting the next phone call. It was Sally Bellis. Once again she received the police report stating that I had called them for the simple reason of not allowing Lisa to take the children out of the house. She told me there was no reason that she could not take them if she wanted to.

"Not when she's drunk she can't," I said.

Sally paused and said, "Oh."

I then said, "I guess it's time for another meeting."

She agreed, and so we arranged to meet the next day. I brought the kids to church thinking that it would be a good place to take them to be surrounded by people who cared about us. When we were all walking towards the church, our minister came up to us and bent down to reassure Krista that everything was going to be fine. I felt the same way now that we were out of the crazy house. I could see the concern on many of the parishioners' faces.

One of my friends came up to me and asked, "What the hell is going on with Lisa? I read about her arrest in the newspaper!" I told him the truth, that she was battling alcoholism. He gave me a hug and wished us all luck. We stayed for a little while after church for the social hour, and then went home to Lisa.

That afternoon I walked over to John and Lynne's house to chat about my upcoming meeting with Miss Bellis. They gave me sound advice which was not to say very much to her. Give her nothing that can be used against you. And do not let either of them know of your future intentions; don't give them any way to plan an assault against you. That was easy, because at this point I did not know what my intentions were. After leaving their house, I felt that I had some control. All I had to do was to remain quiet, and there was nothing DSS could do to hurt me or our family.

BOOZE IN A BABY BOTTLE

The next morning I got Andrew and Krista up and off to school. Robert was in his crib content, so I could focus on the Sally Bellis visit. Earlier that morning, as I was getting the kids' breakfast, I noticed Robert's baby bottle in a strange place in the pantry. I noticed that it was about half full, so I opened the top and took a sniff. It was not formula, but vodka! Lisa's newest hiding place was in Robert's baby bottle. This was so unbelievable to me that she could put her own child at risk for her own self-medication. I made sure that it was hidden out of the way so that it could in no way be used by mistake to feed him. I thought I might need this as evidence when Sally found her usual way of attacking my credibility.

This time I was ready. Before the meeting was to take place, I had spoken to my mother. She asked if she could come over during the meeting to speak to Sally Bellis. I said that I did not know if it would do more harm than good, but I also knew my mother had a lot to get off her mind. So I told her if she really wanted to she could. Sally Bellis once again arrived, and the three of us once again were sitting at the kitchen table. Lisa did not say very much. Sally immediately went on the attack saying that I had overreacted when I called the police. I told her that Lisa had been drunk, and there was no reason for her to take the kids out of our house. She said, "Well maybe it had to do with the letter."

I was not going to react to that statement. At that moment I heard the doorbell ring. I got up and let my mother in. She immediately came into the kitchen and sat down with us.

She looked sternly at Sally Bellis and said, "You know it's you and your department that has caused so much trouble for this family. You are what's wrong with DSS. Don't you know that Lisa is an alcoholic?!"

"You don't know half of what your son has been doing," Sally Bellis replied.

I immediately interrupted the discussion knowing that it was just going to turn into "he said, she said". I said, "Mom, thanks for your input, but you can go now. I do appreciate your help."

She got up and I walked her to the front door. I said thank you and that I would call her later. When I walked back into the room and sat down again Sally said some snide remark about my mother, but I just let it go. She then said, "All right. Now prove to me that Lisa is an alcoholic!"

I stood up from the table and said, "Wait right here."

I walked around the corner and picked up a laundry basket. I then went around to all the places I knew that Lisa liked to hide her booze. I opened up drawers, and into closets, and found vodka, gin, and wine bottles either completely empty or partially full. I was gone for a good 10 minutes without hearing any words coming from the kitchen. The basket was overflowing with bottles. I walked back into the kitchen, and placed the basket on the floor in front of her.

I then said, "Oh wait. I have something else to show you."

I then went into the pantry and grabbed the blue baby bottle, and placed it on the kitchen table in front of both of them. Lisa looked numb. I told Miss Bellis to look inside the bottle. After opening it, she exclaimed, "There is alcohol in this baby bottle! This could kill Robert!" I simply said, "See?"

She looked horrified. The bottles in the laundry basket and the booze in the baby bottle made it impossible for her to blame me any longer.

"So what are your plans now?" Sally asked me.

"I don't know," I said. "I have not made up my mind yet."

At this point I was very worried that Sally Bellis and her team back at the DSS office would make their decision to take away our kids and put them in a foster home. At this point I thought it was a very good possibility, so I decided to go on the offensive.

"So, you know that Lisa is an irresponsible alcoholic mother," I said to her, "and you think that I am an asshole. What are you planning to do with our children? I need to know so that I can go down to their school and let their principal know."

She replied, "I don't know yet. We will have a meeting to determine what course of action to take next."

I said fine, and waited for her to leave our house before I drove to Charlotte Dunning Elementary School to meet with the principal. Upon arriving, I met with the principal privately and with two of the schools guidance counselors. They already knew about the family situation, and were very supportive for the kids' sakes. I told them that there was a very good possibility that all of our kids would be taken to foster homes. There was nothing more any of us could do except hope for the most favorable outcome for the family.

I drove back home. I worked from the house that day waiting for Andrew and Krista to get off the bus. Nothing happened. No phone call came from DSS or from the school. I felt relieved but not out of the woods yet. Anything was possible with DSS. A week went by without a word. By the second week I finally received a phone call from a very pleasant young woman from the DSS office stating that she had been assigned to our family. I asked what happened to Sally Bellis. She said that she did not know. I was dumb-founded, but ecstatic! I yelled happily with my arms raised in the air after I got off the phone. Lisa looked very sad. Her one ally was gone. Everyone else in our inner circle now knew the truth. There was nowhere for her to hide her addiction any longer. Now she would have to face the truth and get help or experience more future legal consequences.

RELIEF

The next weekend I brought our family to watch Andrew play soccer with his team. My brother John showed up, and I gave him the news. For the first time in a very long time I felt the pressure was off my shoulders. He was very happy with the news that Sally Bellis was finally out of our lives. Lisa sat on the grass behind where I was coaching playing with Robert. All appeared right with the world. I told him that I was not sure what my next move was going to be or when. He did not give me any advice. But I knew he was almost relieved as I was. Maybe now we could finally relax and maybe the kids would be safe. The game was soon over, and we left the field as one happy family.

It was strange, but I felt that I was finally in control of my life, as well as my kids'. I did not feel that way about Lisa, because nothing had changed with her. She was still an alcoholic with what appeared no real supervision or consequences. She did continue meeting with her probation officer, but she could "yes" him, and he would feel that he had done his job. I wished that I could speak to him too, but I was still kept away, so I did not know if there was going to be any progress made or how she was going to become sober and stay that way.

A few days later after the woman from DSS had called she arrived at our house. She was young and pretty, and very nice to me. I believe that the DSS board must have held a meeting with Sally Bellis and found that they had been fooled by a very crafty alcoholic, and that I was not the menace that they had made me out to be. They thought it was wiser to remove Miss Bellis from a very volatile situation and bring in a new person that could then close the case without any collateral damage being done to their organization.

The young woman in her mid 20's sat down with us to say that we had to go forward with the recommendation of DSS and begin our weekly meetings with SMOC's Family Services program. We would each meet with a trained therapist, and work out our family issues so that we could improve how our family would get along in the future. Part of me knew that this was never going to change how Lisa abused alcohol, and that she would just toy with this new person just as she had with all the others. But I was going to do whatever it took to remove DSS from our house once and for all. If it meant working with a couple of naïve women, then I could play the game too.

The woman that I was assigned to was in her 30's and did not take any crap. She was here to work to make things better in my relationship with my family. This time I did not say very much, except when asked a question or if she wanted me to give my side of the story. I did not embellish, I just spoke my mind. I knew she was feeling me out to see if I was giving her a bunch of bull or if I was for real. I did not mind meeting with her, because I knew that she was not jaded by what she knew of our case. She wanted nothing but the truth, and so did I. We were on the same page. I was going to learn something from her, and early on I did. At one point in my relationship with Andrew, whenever I sat down with him to help with his homework, he would immediately become angry. He liked to swear at me. It was his way of getting me angry, so that it would interfere with what he was supposed to be doing. I would then fall right into it and get madder by the minute. In the end I would chase him up to his bedroom for a time out. This action only made me feel bad about myself, and he won out in not finishing his homework.

My therapist's suggestion was the next time he started with the naughty talk, just say, "Sorry Andrew. If you continue to speak to me that way, then I cannot help you with your homework." And then leave the room, so that he had to take ownership of his bad behavior.

The next time I tried to help him he went right into his usual antics. I said what I had to say, and then left the room without raising my voice or chasing him to his room. It worked like a charm. He looked at me in amazement, and within a few minutes he was working on his homework on his own without any fuss. I was thrilled, and felt that I had learned a very important lesson.

Lisa's therapist was an older woman in her mid 50's. They got along very well. Lisa appeared to be doing better, and so everything was going along very smoothly. The time with these two women lasted about a month. In the end we met at our house, and said our good-by's and gave them hugs. We were appreciative of their guidance, but I was glad this phase was over. We met with the staff at DSS one last time, and they agreed to close the case on Lisa. I felt that nothing had been accomplished in treating Lisa. All that had occurred was that I was no longer looked upon as the villain. Lisa had been slowed by the agency, but she was still allowed to continue her crazy lifestyle. I was hoping that since she had been caught in all her lies that she would think twice about drinking so blatantly again. I still felt very much alone. At least I was not under attack any longer.

EASY WAY

We had been living with only one vehicle for the past three months. I liked driving the minivan, because it felt like a mobile office. Sometimes I would pull over before an appointment and do paperwork in the second row of seats. I liked being a "van guy", and it was a very reliable one. I was glad that if Lisa had to total a car it was not the minivan, especially when we used it with the kids all the time. We could get up to move back with the kids if there was a skirmish going on. But Lisa was now putting pressure on me to buy another vehicle. She had gone through the alcohol program assigned by the courts. The law was that first time DUI offenders—if they finished the mandatory program and remained alcohol free for 90 days—would have the DUI charge struck from their driving records and their licenses would be reinstated. Lisa had met those requirements, and so had her record expunged. Now, armed with her license, she was once again free to drive.

I was not happy, because I knew that without any supervision, she would continue to drink. I did not believe that even the thought of a second DUI looming over her head that would slow her down. I truly wished that the loss of her license would have been for a year, and in that way I could relax and not worry about her driving my kids or hurting other drivers. That would send a much stronger message to the offender that the courts really took drunk driving seriously. But the law is the law, and so I had to accept the outcome.

 Lisa began to ask when I was going to look to buy another car. I thought she had a lot of gall asking me such a question, since she had totaled my Honda just a few months ago. I knew that she was trying to get her freedom back and not be stuck at home all day with nothing to do. I enjoyed having only one car, and one car payment, as well as insurance protection for only one car. My costs had been reduced dramatically, and I still had the money from the insurance company that was earmarked for my next car. What I was hoping was that she would get a part time job to help pay for the new car, as well as pay down her Ebay debt. That wish was not in her thought process.

 I told her that I would really appreciate it if she would go online and research Honda Accords to check out what new deals there were. She was more than happy to do that. That was my first mistake. I had never bought such an important purchase over the Internet, but I was tired of the sales pressure from the dealerships that I had been to in the past. It always took hours, and then I still walked away feeling ripped off. I felt it was Lisa's duty to help resolve this issue. I had forgotten that my cousin Tim was married to a crazy woman who was addicted to drugs, and when he put her in charge of the household finances chaos soon ensued. But this is where my denial got the best of me. Lisa did find an inexpensive Honda Accord through a dealership by way of an online buying source. I bought it sight and driving unseen, and had to go to a dealership in Brookline to pick it up. When I got in the car I found that it did not have power windows or door locks. It was the stripped down version of anything that I would ever want to buy. Now for the next 5 years I was stuck with payments and with a car that I was not happy with!

Lisa went back to driving the minivan, and was very happy to be free to go as she pleased. I had tried to take the easy way out, but in the end it cost me my joy and comfort of owning a new car. I felt like a victim, because I had put a woman with a sickness in charge of important aspects of my life in trying to teach her a lesson, but in the end it was I who learned a very valuable lesson. Lisa felt like she had done something worthy, but in a crazy way that had affected me negatively. She was now off the hook once again. I felt even if she was to drive drunk again, and lose her license again, that the courts would enable her again. I knew that I was running out of options, and my next decision would not only be a drastic one, but would change our family forever. I was hoping that the day would never come that I would have to make such a decision. The saying, "Some of God's greatest gifts are from unanswered prayers" was coming sooner than I had anticipated, and I was going to have to make the most difficult decision of my life.

OPENING WOUNDS

In January of 2002 the press was having a field day exposing priests who had molested children in their parish over many years. One by one the victims came out years after they had experienced such trauma as youths trusting the hierarchy of their church. It took great courage to come out as the now-adult children and to testify against these monsters. But at the same time it also opened up the wounds of Lisa's childhood. She could not hide from her past. She also learned from one of her good friends that her daughter had been molested by a teacher while living in another country. That just added fuel to her already struggling with addiction. She began to drink more and more to drown out the visions in her head. By March she was swamped in her own misery, and like quicksand, the more she struggled with her disease the worse it became.

I had my mother come over as much as she could to look in on Lisa and young Robert while I was at work. I knew something had to be done, and soon. My kids were in danger. I did not want to call DSS because I knew, with a third open case against Lisa, that our kids would be removed from the house. I decided to call Lisa's doctor and bring him up to speed as to how bad her drinking had become. He suggested that I call Newton Wellesley Hospital again to find out if there were any beds available. As I was on the phone, Andrew came into the kitchen to let me know that mom had left the house and he did not know where she had gone. I told the doctor I had to go, and that I would report back to him later that day.

Andrew and I went outside to see if the minivan was still in the driveway. It was. There was no sign of her. I put all the kids in the minivan, and we drove up the road towards my parents' house. She was nowhere to be seen. I doubled back, and drove past my brother's house towards the railroad tracks and the Mass Pike overpass. In the corner of our eyes we saw Lisa walking on the train bridge towards an area that was slightly open over the turnpike. I squealed onto the tracks, and bolted out of the car. Both Andrew and I ran up to her and put our arms around her to stop her.

"Let me go! Let me go!" she moaned. "I can't do this anymore!"

Andrew and I kept saying that everything was going to be ok as we walked her back to the minivan. Once we got home, I called the doctor and told him that we had found Lisa walking on a train bridge, and was possibly thinking about committing suicide. He told me to call the MetroWest Medical Center and have her committed for the night. We could then figure out where she would go from there. After calling my parents to have them look after the kids, I drove with Lisa to downtown Framingham to the hospital. I had already called the emergency room to let them know her condition. Upon arriving the nurses took her right in, so that they could process her, and then take her vital signs. I stayed with her for an hour, and then thought it would be best to let her detox with people who knew what they were doing. I asked the head nurse to call me later that evening to discuss what options we had with her. I then walked over to the nearby Friendly's where my parents had taken the kids for dinner. My dad had already ordered me a cheeseburger, so I got to decompress, but I was very scared. I did not have any idea where all this was heading.

After dinner, I drove the kids home and put them to bed. At around 2 a.m. the phone rang. It was the nurse that I had met earlier. She asked me about Lisa. I told her that she had been thinking about suicide, but it was more of a cry for help, and I did not think she needed to be committed, but did need a place that could focus on her alcohol abuse. She said that they had contacted AdCare in Worcester, that they had a bed for her, and would pick her up in the morning.

I was ecstatic! I told the nurse that this was just what Lisa needed and maybe now she could face her demons. I woke up the next morning at 8:00, and made breakfast. A few minutes later Lisa called and asked if I would pick her up from the hospital, because no one was checking in on her.

"I can't," I said "because someone from AdCare Hospital is going to pick you up."

She said that she was bored, and wanted to come home. I told her to stay put, and not to go anywhere. I hung up the phone thinking that the nurses would be there to speak to her, and calm her fears, and that she would then be picked up and cared for properly. But at 10:00 while I was cleaning up in the kitchen I heard the front door open. It was Lisa! As she came in, I looked at her with shock. She was holding her overnight gear. I was hoping that she was just stopping by to pick up a few items before she left for the hospital. She said that she had waited long enough, so she decided to walk home.

"You have to go back now," I told her "or you will miss your opportunity to ride to AdCare!"

She just looked at me. I immediately called the hospital to find out what was going on. I spoke to the head nurse on duty. She said that the staff from AdCare had come to pick her up, but because she was not there, they left.

"What should I do now?" I asked.

She said there was nothing they could do, because Lisa had lost the bed available for her. I was devastated. Lisa had walked the three miles home, and in so doing lost her chance at getting well. I had only one option left and that was to call Connections to see if they could talk sense to her, and maybe help steer her in the right direction.

CONNECTIONS ~

I called the staff at Connections to set up a meeting with us to figure out what to do next. Lisa liked going to her counselors there because she could tell her stories about her terrible abusive home life, and they gladly believed her. This time though the atmosphere was different. They knew that Lisa had crossed the line into uncontrolled addictive behavior, and they were ready for her. The two counselors sat us down and said that it was time for Lisa to get some real help away from home. They had a recommendation to have her admitted to a place called Serenity House located just a few miles away in Hopkinton. They said it was time for her to completely focus on her sobriety in a safe environment. They knew that she could no longer cope with her responsibilities as a mother, and now had to work on herself.

The woman said, "We even see a difference in Tom". I did not know what she was talking about. I had only been to a couple of meetings with them and Lisa, so how would they know anything about my behavior? I felt I had always been there for her and had tried my damndest to help her get sober. But the fact that they now appeared to "get it", I felt I now had the backing to get her well.

The counselor had a form admitting her to the facility all filled out. All Lisa had to do was sign it. I asked what the cost was going to be, and they said $500 per month. I thought that was well worth the price to save her life, our family, and our marriage. But she balked at the whole idea of leaving her children behind. She knew that I did not want her mother in our house any longer interfering with my parenting or my sanity. I quickly said that I would be fair allowing both grandmothers to help out periodically when I felt I needed help. The counselors were insistent that she sign the forms, and give in to getting the help that would put her back on the road to sobriety. She finally acquiesced and signed the forms.

I was jumping for joy inside. I told them that we would drive to Serenity House to check it out and meet the staff today. We brought the kids with us, as we drove up the long wooded road. It was a very pleasant rustic but modern house. The staff greeted us enthusiastically, and the first question that was asked was, "What is your addiction?" Lisa stated, "Alcohol." The woman just nodded, and then walked us around. The place felt very homey, and I tried to be as positive as I could. I told the kids that this was where mom was going to stay for a while, but we would all visit as much as we could. Lisa did not look thrilled. In fact, she gave no visible sign of acceptance. I wanted to know when Lisa could gain admittance there. The woman said that they had to make sure that she was sober before she did, then they could begin the process of truly keeping her that way. After leaving there, I called up the counselor at Connections to say that we had seen the house, but I had one big concern, and that was would she really be willing to be admitted? If she had to go to get detoxed, then there was a very good chance that she would decide not to go because she would feel fine again.

"Don't worry," the counselor said. "We'll make sure she gets there."

I felt like they had my back, but I knew there was no way they could force her to go there. I did not believe that this was going to happen, even though the denial part of me thought it might. It did not take long for alcohol to take over Lisa's life again. I called Dr. Smith to let him know that she was at it again, and he said that he was ready to help. He had already called The Faulkner Hospital in Boston. They had a bed ready for her, and I called my parents to look after the kids while I was gone for the rest of the day. Lisa did not put up much of a fight, so she packed and was ready to go in less than an hour. When we arrived at the hospital, the nurses were very pleasant and supportive. The hospital was clean and modern and was not depressing. Lisa was happy with her single room, and I was relieved that she was going to be there for a while. I told the nurse there that the plan was that she was going to get sober, and then she would be heading to Serenity House. I thought that if they knew what the plan was, then it would make the transition that much easier. I was hoping that they would talk up the plan that we had set up for her, and that would make it easier to sell her on the transition to her temporary new home in Hopkinton. During the end of the week the hospital invited me and the kids to meet with her and other families that were going through similar experiences.

After Andrew's soccer game ended on that Saturday, we

headed to meet up with her. Lisa was very happy to see the children. She was all smiles, and I was happy that she was sober once again, but at the same time very concerned that she would convince herself out of going where she was expected to go. She was due to be released the following day, so in my mind I had to figure out how we were going to make a brief pit stop at our house, and then drive the few miles to "the house". I picked her up on Sunday after breakfast, and drove back to Framingham. While driving home I tried to make one final feeble attempt at convincing her that going to Serenity House was the right thing to do to ensure her future sobriety. She listened, but said nothing. My heart was sinking as we got closer to home. We both walked into the house, and all I wanted to do was go straight up to our bedroom to help her organize her belongings for the extended stay she was going to have.

She walked directly into the kitchen and said, "I am not going".

"But you have to," I replied. "You agreed to go!"

She then said that she did not trust me in allowing her mother to help out. I said that it was not her concern, and that I would be fair. I said the kids were counting on her to get well and stay sober. She had made up her mind, and was not going anywhere. As I walked out of the kitchen onto the deck, I said, "You will rue the day". I was completely shattered, but saw this coming from the beginning.

The rest of the day I tried to keep busy with house chores and preparing for work the next day. The following day when I arrived at work, I immediately called the head woman counselor at Connections and explained to her that Lisa had decided not to go. Now what were we going to do to change her mind? The woman on the other end of the line said that she agreed with Lisa's decision, and that she was doing fine now. I was totally confused. How could they feel last week that it was imperative that she go to a safe environment away from her family to now forgetting everything that was said and signed? I felt that they had let my entire family down, and especially for letting Lisa off the hook. They had no balls, and no backbone to back up what they had recommended just days earlier. I lost total respect for the organization, and once again I felt they had placed me in a very adversarial position with Lisa. It was Lisa and Connections against me and my kids. How dare They! As with all the other detox organizations they were nothing more than patsies and pawns against the false strength of an alcoholic. Once again I was being forced to take matters into my own hands.

DECISION TIME

I had already been speaking to a few different lawyers about my situation. Each one was more than happy to represent me. I knew that any one of them would be good counsel, but I also knew it would be a very difficult decision to move forward. The outcome was not guaranteed to go in my favor. If anything went wrong I could lose my kids, my house, and everything that mattered to me. Lisa was such a good actress that whoever she chose as her lawyer would fight for her to the end. She would make me look like an abusive husband and father. Even though I had plenty of facts with the backing of a 10-page report I had written for DSS, it was still going to be my word against hers. Who would the judge believe? I knew the answer to that question. I was so stuck in a mess that I could not fix, that I was being pushed by the universe to make a terrible decision that was probably not going to go my way.

I called up Luke my lawyer, to whom I had reached out originally when I was fighting with DSS. He said, "Tom, it's time to shit or get off the pot!"

I felt like I was wasting his time. So I told him that I would get back to him later. I did not want to move forward because it would mean I would have to begin my second divorce proceedings, and that was not what I wanted to do in my heart. Later in the week I called Rebecca who specialized in working with men in difficult divorce situations. She said that she would be ready to go any time because my kids needed protection. They were in danger.

I then met with another attorney who was a client as well as a divorce attorney. He gave me a reality check as to what to expect. He said that I would have to pay child support and possibly alimony. Our house would probably have to be sold if we went 50/50 in our agreement. I would lose a good percentage of time with my children, because it would be a real long shot if I were to get a judgment of full custody of the children. It just does not happen in the Massachusetts court. There would be a guardian ad litem (GAL) assigned if there was any dispute as to which parent should have custody of the kids. And if the custody case went to trial, not only would it be very expensive, but there was a very good chance that the jury would side with Lisa. I said thank you for telling me like it is, and I left knowing that I was not going to pursue divorcing Lisa, because the outcome was too dire. I drove back to my Wellesley office, and was ready to get to work. I felt a great weight had been taken off my shoulders, and I would just figure some other way out of my mess.

DECISION CHANGED ∾

After I arrived at work, I walked into my dad's office to say hi. He pulled out a check. I looked at it for a moment. It was a bankers check for $10,000 that mom had withdrawn from her investment account. It was written to Rebecca Ray the lawyer whom I had met with earlier in the month. My dad said it was for the initial fee to begin the divorce process. My brother John and our parents had been talking and were convinced that this was the only way out of my crazy situation since Lisa was unwilling to get the help that she needed. I was completely taken aback. I was not ready in my mind to take such a jump off the legal abyss, but now I had a big decision to make. I went from being adamant about my decision not to go forward to doing a complete 180 in the other direction. This was a decision completely out of my comfort zone. I had been putting off having to make any hasty moves, because I had no idea of the outcome except that it just did not feel right. But if I did move forward, it was to be an act of courage more than anything, because I felt as if I were sacrificing my future happiness to force my wife to change her behavior, and of course to keep my kids safe. I felt that the decision had been made for me, and that if I did not take this drastic step then I never would.

    I asked a friend at work what he thought, and he said that he had faith in my decision, and whatever I decided to do was the right way to go. I found out later that he too was married to an alcoholic, but he had decided to stay married and have faith in the Al-Anon 12-step program. This move forward was more than an act of tough love, but it was time to take a stand against an enemy that had taken countless lives and ruined families. It was me against the disease with the help of an enabling legal system. But my excuses were gone. I now had the financial backing of my mom and dad and the loving support of my brother and sister-in-law. I had to find the inner strength to take that leap of faith. It surprised me how quickly I did an about face. Instead of taking the easy way out and going back for more frustration, I now had decided to send the check to my lawyer. The main reason I decided to go ahead with the divorce was the fact that if my family felt so strongly to protect my kids from their own mother, that I had no other choice. Otherwise, I would be letting them down, and keeping my kids in constant danger. I thought I should take the check home with me and give myself one more day to think it over. But I knew what I had to do.

SENDING OFF THE CHECK

The next morning when I arrived at work, I wrote a note to go along with the $10,000 check to my attorney, sealed the envelope and walked it up to the receptionist at the front desk to be mailed. As I handed her the envelope I said, "This is the saddest day of my life." She asked why? I told her what I was about to take on. She said that she too had gone through a painful divorce, but in the end it was worth it. I felt a little bit of relief, but inside I was very sad that I was about to divorce a woman that I still loved. I could not see any other alternative. Lisa was adamant that she no longer needed help of any kind. The disease had won and completely taken over her sense of responsibility to her own family. I could not be a party to her madness. The safety of my kids was paramount. I had to do what her mother did not have the courage to do years earlier. I knew this was not going to make me any kind of hero, in fact I knew that I would end up being the villain, especially if things did not go my way in court. I knew the odds were stacked against me, but I went forward anyway. Now all I had to do was bide my time and wait for my attorney to contact me, and lead me through this mess.

 I did trust her, and I knew she had my back, but it was the system that I did not trust. I had witnessed firsthand the dysfunctional world of DSS, which was a very good indicator of what a government program was unable to do, and that was to truly help a family in crisis. They went by a set of antiquated guidelines that in the real world did not help the situation, but only made matters worse by enabling the sick member of the household. I was truly hoping that the judge would see through to the truth, and in the end give me full custody of my children so that Lisa's hand would be forced to get the help she needed if she wanted to have a normal relationship with our kids. My goal was to have full control over this insanity once and for all, and then to have Lisa get sober, and finally to take her back into our marital home once she was free of alcoholism. This was a long shot, because I knew that if she became pissed off and scared, she might go the opposite way and be ruthless.

My big fear was who she would hire as her counsel. I knew my character would be attacked in court, and if the judge and jury believed her story of me the abusive husband, then the probability of me ending up out of the house was real. My mind had to almost go numb, so that I could move forward in this endeavor or else I would not go through with it. If I did nothing, then Lisa would just keep drinking with no consequences, and it would be just a matter of time before something terrible happened to one of my kids. And it already had. I had already lived through it. Nothing was going to change unless I stopped going into denial. Even though I did not feel in the least confident in my decision, I felt as if the universe was pushing me forward, and that this time I had to see this decision through to the end.

I called my attorney at the end of the week to make sure she had received the check. She had, and she then gave me a list of things to obtain for her. One was to go down to the town hall and obtain a copy of our marriage license, which I did. That is when it began to hit home that I was really going through with this. My mind was numb to the whole process, but I did whatever my attorney told me to do. I also set up a meeting with her and asked if my brother could attend the meeting just to make sure I was not missing anything in translation about the divorce proceedings. I needed a sign of some kind to help assure me that I was on the right track. As I walked away from my car in the Government Center Parking Lot, I somehow flipped up a penny from the ground with my right foot. It then landed on the top of my left shoe! I guess I got the sign!

I met John in the lawyer's office and it was the same day that my father had another heart episode and was taken to the hospital in Framingham. I thought it might be a good idea to cancel the meeting, but it turned out to be a minor issue with his heart, and he would be fine. So I kept the meeting on. We all sat down together, and my attorney asked what questions I had for her. I asked her what chance I had in actually getting full custody of my kids. She said that it would take a lot to swing the pendulum in my favor. She was also matter-of-fact in stating that my child support obligation would be about $30,000 per year.

I said, "How am I going to afford that?"

She just said, "Stay the course."

Again, the safety of my kids was on the line. She wanted me to get the records from DSS, so that she could build our case. I knew this was not going to be easy, because they had been so secretive and deceitful when I was dealing with them directly. But this gave me some breathing room to take in all that had been said to me.

John said that he was never " more sure" of anything in his life than for me to get a divorce from this crazy woman. I could not disagree with him. I just needed time to wrap my brain around this ordeal that I was bringing onto myself and my family. John was very impressed with my attorney and felt confident that I was well represented. My lawyer said to us that if Lisa was truly trying to get sober, then she would be going to AA meetings daily, and the fact that she had blown a 3.0 on the breathalyzer after hitting a telephone pole was a very good indicator of just how far into the disease she had gone. I wanted to know the outcome of all this. I wanted guarantees that my life would be unscathed, and that I would not lose everything, especially not my kids. I wanted reassurance that I would survive after the dust had settled. My fantasy was that Lisa would see how strong I was, and that I had stood up to her, and that she would fall back in love with me for my strength and courage. I had to believe that the judge would read the records and have no choice but to give me full custody, while Lisa went to a half way house. We could then be a happy family once again. I was trying to see this legal situation from every angle. I wanted to leave no stone unturned, so that I would not be blindsided by something that I had missed because I had not thought of it or asked a simple question. If anything went wrong, then it could lead to years of misery. I had the support of my family, my friends, and lawyer, and my therapist. I had it all.

STAYING THE COURSE

I had uncertainty in my gut which would not go away. My lawyer called me during the week to let me know that she had received the marriage license. Now all we had to do was go to court. The following Monday she called me at work to let me know that we would be going to court the next day. I was very scared of what was coming. I was not happy about turning my entire family upside down. That was the handiwork of Lisa. My job had always been to right the sinking ship. Now I was heading straight into the storm knowing that I would be swept in every direction. The following day my lawyer called again. But this time she said that we were not going to court because there was a crazy judge presiding, and that he was so unpredictable that it was not worth taking a chance for his verdict to go against us. I was so relieved that I began crying to myself. My lawyer said the best thing to do was to delay going to court until there was a different judge, a more reasonable judge to plead our case.

The long Memorial Day weekend was coming up, so I asked her what I should do. She said, "Go to Mattapoisett with the family and enjoy yourself." I thought I would have to be a great actor, and so would my parents, so that we did not let the cat out of the bag. We had to pretend that all was normal when, in fact, the world was about to come off its' axis.

We actually had a wonderful time on our mini vacation. At one point I wanted to go for a long walk with my mother to let her know that I had changed my mind, and that I was not going through with the vacate order and divorce proceedings. Something inside me told me not to say anything and just remain silent. So I never said a word to either of my parents about how I felt. I just stayed the course. At one point all three of our kids surrounded Lisa and all hugged her at the same time. She looked like she had been through a war and did not look like she was on the road to recovery. I did not see her even trying to get sober. I did not bother looking for her stash of booze any more, because I did not see the point. She was an active alcoholic who had been through rehab time after time, and there was nothing more that I could do to help her except throw a monkey wrench right into addiction.

I was about to hear a lot of sparks fly. I spoke to some of my cousins about my situation, and they too were very supportive of my decision. There was nothing anyone could do to help our family except the legal system at this point. At one point I wanted to tell Lisa what was about to take place, but that would take away any options that I had. I wanted her to see what the rest of us saw. I wanted her to miraculously get well and stop the insanity that was never-ending. I was getting so frustrated that when Lisa and the kids and I walked through the boat yard I began yelling at her saying, "Why won't you get the help you need?" She just stared at me like I was nuts. I felt so confused and powerless. I wanted to do something—anything—to fix all of this, but there was nothing I could do to change her. The next court date was on the horizon, and I would have to follow through for the safety of my kids and for the sake of my sanity. My entire family had been through enough, and I was the only one that could make this very difficult grown up decision.

GOING TO COURT

Krista's birthday was on the 8th of June, so we decided to have a small party with her friends at our neighborhood pool. Lisa looked angry the entire time, like the world was on her shoulders. I did not stay long because I had to coach Andrew's soccer team. Everything felt different, as if there was a seismic shift in our universe. I was still looking for a miracle, but one never came. The following Monday I received a phone call from my attorney saying, "We are going to court tomorrow, so get ready, and bring your check book!"

I called my parents and my brother John to let him know what was happening. I needed their support now more than ever. I truly felt as though I was walking off a cliff, and not knowing how far down I was heading. I felt like someone else was now controlling my life, and I did not like feeling out of control. My plan for the kids was to have them go to school, and then I would meet them there and have a meeting with their guidance counselors and the school principal to let them know what was happening, and that we were truly just trying to help Lisa deal with her addiction. I was going to have my mother accompany me back to my house, so that there would be a witness to whatever reaction Lisa was going to have when I handed her eviction and divorce papers. I knew she would be shocked and angry, and I did not want the kids to witness this event.

That morning when I woke up, I walked into the bathroom and while looking in the mirror I said, "It is going to be a great day." I am sure I did not really believe my words, but I needed to do something to psych myself up, to keep myself from losing my courage, and to keep moving forward. I went back into our bedroom and saw Lisa poke her head up with Robert snuggled next to her under the covers and give me a small smile. At that point I truly wanted to tell her what was about to take place, but once again I kept my mouth shut.

I said good-by to her and the kids, and drove off to Cambridge to meet up with my attorney by 9 a.m. My mind was numb as I drove. Nothing felt right, but I kept driving. When I met up with her I said that I did not think this was the right course of action to take. She just kept reassuring me that it was the right thing to do and that it was time to sign forms and then wait until our name was called to go in front of the judge. My attorney had made sure that it was a new judge to whom we would plead our case, and so for a moment I felt relief, and felt that I was being counseled in the right way. We met with the judge for a very brief amount of time to explain that it was in the best interest of my children that my wife be vacated from the home. The judge wondered why the other party was not present, and we told her that she was not of sound mind to do so. The judge agreed with our vacate order, but said that the following Monday she wanted to meet with

Lisa also to determine if this order should be upheld.

I was very fearful of that, because I knew Lisa would hire a sympathetic attorney who would believe whatever stories she told about me. I would be attacked and have to prove my side of the case. This was not going to be pretty. We left the court house with two vacate order forms. One copy I had to leave off at the Framingham Police Station and the other I had to keep with me at all times, so if the police came to our house and questioned me, then I would have legal protection.

After leaving the police station, I drove to my parent's house to pick up my mother. We then drove to my house, and as we pulled in the driveway Lisa was just pulling out. She saw us and smiled and then drove back in. I got out of the car and walked over to her saying that we needed to go inside to talk. I became weepy, but I stayed together long enough to hand her the vacate order and to tell her that she had to leave the house this afternoon unless she agreed to go to Serenity House today.

She just shook her head and said, "I can't believe you are doing this! Fuck you! I want a divorce!"

She left the kitchen and went upstairs to make a few phone calls to her friends and to her support group at Connections. I told my mother it was time to go, so I drove her back to her house, and then went to Charlotte Dunning to pick up Andrew and Krista. Robert was still at the day care at the center of town, so we picked him up also. As we were driving back to the house, I noticed that Lisa's car was still in the driveway. She had not left the house yet. I was not sure if the constable had delivered the forms to her after I had been away for a few hours. I turned around and went back to my parent's house to call my attorney to tell her that Lisa had not left yet. She told me to call the police station to make sure that she was to leave at once. A little while later I called Lynne to find out if Lisa had driven away. She said that there was no car in the driveway.

I felt relieved and sad all at the same time. I could not believe that I had actually gone through with kicking my wife out of the house. All the trust between us was gone, and so to was our marriage. I was glad that I had the kids safely with me, but I knew that they would miss their mother terribly. I tried to keep things as normal as I could, but I could see just how sad Andrew was already. All I wanted was this nightmare to be over, but it was far from it. Next week, I would be going in front of the judge and sitting across from me would be Lisa and her attorney, and nothing more than a miracle could make things right again.

NIGHTMARE BEGINS

That night I made the kids dinner, and tried to have some normalcy, but without their mother nothing felt normal. Andrew was very upset and lay face down on his bed crying. At that point all I wanted to do was erase everything that had just occurred—even to go back to the insanity— but I just talked to the kids saying that this was all for the best and was to help mommy get well. I did not feel good about the prospects of having to go back into court in front of an angry alcoholic, her nasty lawyer, and a sympathetic judge. I did not trust the system or the advice from anyone. My gut was making me feel very uncomfortable like somehow this whole mess was my fault, which I knew was classic enabling for the alcoholic. All I wanted was closure from this continuous nightmare, but I knew much more was to come unless the judge was in favor of our decision to have Lisa permanently removed from the marital home and made to go to a long term alcohol recovery facility. That is what I was hoping for, but it was all completely out of my hands.

Lisa had tried calling to speak with the kids. I told her that until this situation was resolved she could not, and I hung up on her. Over the weekend I ran up and down the street to help relieve some of the tension I was feeling. I did not want to travel very far, because I was in total charge of the children, and I feared she might show up unannounced, and that would make things worse. I had no idea where Lisa was staying, but I did know that she was very clever and resourceful, and that she was getting ready any way she could for her court date. I made sure that there was money in our joint checking account in case she needed to stay in a motel. I knew that she was scared and unprepared for what I had done, and this made me very nervous. She could easily pull out all the stops, and say and do anything that was necessary to get back in the house, and remove her only adversary. I wanted to try and play fair, but that had ended the moment I had her removed from her kids.

That next Monday we were scheduled to be back in court. I got the kids on the bus, and made arrangements for my mom to look after Robert. I drove into Cambridge with my father for moral support. I still felt extremely uncomfortable like I was going into a kangaroo court with no experience on how to present my side of the story. I had to leave this up to my attorney who seemed very confident in what she was doing. Sitting outside the courtroom, we met up with her and sat on a bench next to each other while she filled us in to what was going to happen.

Soon Lisa entered and she had made sure she looked presentable and well dressed. She was followed by her attorney, her mother, and a very tall woman who represented Connections counselors. This was her support system. All the people I despised and had no respect for were now just a few feet away from me. I felt like good and evil were in the same room about to do battle, and I was not prepared to lose to these people. Both lawyers greeted each other with a handshake, and I tried my best to ignore Lisa and especially her stoic mother. I had done my best to remove her from my life, and now she was back in my face at the most difficult time in my life. It felt so contradictory that her mother who had not been there to protect Lisa as a child was now acting like she cared and was backing her. It made me feel like barfing, but I had to remain strong and know that I was doing the right thing for my kids.

After a few minutes of discussing our case, we all went into the courtroom. We sat on the right side of the room, and Lisa and her entourage sat in the middle. I kept looking over and then looking away. Finally we were called up in front of the judge who was a woman in her forties. She reviewed the transcripts that depicted our case. She wanted to know the reason for having Lisa vacated from the premises. My lawyer explained the history of her drinking, driving drunk, and the two DSS cases that had been opened on her.

Then it was Lisa's lawyer's turn to explain their side. She went on and on about how her client had been working very hard to remain sober and to get help and attend weekly meetings at Connections. After she was done, my attorney said that Lisa needed to go to a long-term facility to get the real help she needed. Lisa's attorney said that I should be removed from the marital home due to my abusive behavior towards her client. I did not see that logic coming my way. I was relieved when the judge dismissed that recommendation.

But then the judge asked Lisa if she had a place that she could live while this case was being determined. First she asked if she could live with her mother. She said no because her mother lived in a one-bedroom apartment. Then she asked if she could live with her father. She said no because he lived too far away, and he was not a well man. Lisa explained that she had been living in a local motel while vacated from her home. The judge said that in her view that Lisa should be allowed back in her home, but with conditions that she must follow with direction from the court. I could not believe that the judge thought it was a good idea to have two people that did not trust or like each other at this time to live under the same roof, especially when the final outcome was going to be a divorce!

My lawyer tried vehemently to explain to the judge that this was a very bad idea, and that Lisa needed real long term counseling.

"What we have here is a raging alcoholic," the judge said, "but I feel it is in the best interest of all to have her back in the marital home with her children."

The judge then ordered a court officer meet with us to go over the requirements to have Lisa tested weekly by way of a random urine test by a disinterested third party. Her attorney asked if Connections counseling could do the testing due to their close proximity. The other would be in Wellesley, and because she had only 20 minutes to get to a facility after receiving the phone call from the court, I thought it was a fair request and agreed. I was also given the authority to take Lisa to the local police station to have a hair follicle test done if I suspected her drinking. My first thought was how was I going to convince or force her to go down to the police station to get this test done when she knew it meant the loss of being with her children. I knew this was putting me into a very volatile situation, but I still went along with it.

In the end I received full custody of my children, and I was thankful for that, but at the same time I had to live with a vindictive person who had once been the love of my life. I was glad on one hand that we were going to live as a family unit again, but I also knew that this could not possibly work out because Lisa still needed to drink, and I was a major impediment to that.

We were assigned a Guardian Ad Litem (GAL) recommended by my lawyer who had great luck with him in the past with other cases. The other attorney said that would be fine, and we soon left the courthouse. I was thankful that this crazy ordeal was over, but now I had to go home and meet Lisa there. This was going to be a very tense time. I was nervous that while I was away at work during the day that she would have a free hand to do whatever she could to torture me by having access to credit cards, Ebay, and whatever else she could do to ruin me financially. Nothing had really changed except that she was angrier towards me, and that the lack of affection, and the increase of tension was going to do a job on my psyche. I had to focus on what I was to do, as well as on my kids. When she came into the house that afternoon, I gave her a hug and tried to hand out an olive branch of truce, but nothing felt right. Again I hoped for another miracle.

LIVING TOGETHER SEPARATELY

The very strange part of all this was that we were living as a family, but separately all at the same time. Lisa's attorney said that I would have to leave the marital bedroom. This was the moment when I felt as though I was being punished for my actions. Why was I supposed to be removed from the bedroom? It was Lisa's drinking and illegal behavior that had gotten us into this mess in the first place, and already I was being forced out. I knew I could not sleep next to her, so I decided to sleep next to Andrew in his room. There were two beds in there, and I was going to keep my clothes in my closet so I would not have to be too disrupted while this crazy time was occurring. After my attorney and I had stepped out of the courtroom, she revealed to me that she had heard that the judge was a recovering alcoholic and had empathy for the defendant.

I was shocked that we had waited for another judge to take the bench because the first was a loon, and then to find out this judge took the side of the alcoholic because she was one too! When I was speaking to Lisa one day out of frustration I blurted out that she had been very lucky that the judge had taken her side due to the fact that she was a recovering alcoholic, and that kept her from getting the real help she needed. This was not a good move on my part, because Lisa was crazy like a fox, and would probably use this against me somehow. My attorney had stated that anything I said to her would be handing over ammunition she needed on a silver platter. I felt very resentful that I had to watch everything I said or did around her. We should have been living apart during this time, but instead I was living in the middle of the lion's den. I still had to go to work and make money to pay for everything. I felt like dead man walking, because I had to keep up a façade of happiness and positivity on the outside, so that I could obtain and sell new clients life insurance. My production went down, but I was lucky to have renewals and cash value that I would need to borrow on from my life insurance to pay for part of the legal bills that were coming my way. My dad helped to pay for the major part of these bills. This was going to get expensive, for not only was I getting the beating of the emotional side of the legal system, but even more importantly the financial side as well.

While the days went by Lisa and I still had to parent our three children. That meant going places together, and pretending to be a solid family. I kept hoping that somehow Lisa would see the light, and we could put a stop to this madness. When I spoke to our neighbors, I told them what was happening, and how I wished for reconciliation. They all had empathy for me, but there was nothing they could do, and in the end they would listen to Lisa's side anyway. The random alcoholic urine testing was supposed to commence right away, but no one called from the court for over two weeks. This was probably due to the back-log of cases, as well as being the summer vacation time.

I called my attorney to let her know, and she called the Middlesex court. A few days later Lisa received her first call from the court, and she drove herself down to Connections for her urine test. Of course it came out negative. I had no proof whether or not she was drinking, because her appearance had not changed all that much. She constantly looked a bit disheveled and a tad shaky, but I did not want to use up my one ace in the hole to take her down to the police station. I was worried that I would look like I was crying wolf, and that this would be used against me when we were to either face the GAL or the judge. I hoped that Connections would be fair about their testing, and that they would watch her closely pee. But I did not truly believe that they could play by the rules. Lisa was their trophy, and there was no way they would let her fail.

URINE FOUND ∾

Connections needed a hero and a success story so that they could keep their doors open. Lisa was the perfect foil. She was beautiful with her everlasting smile. She was smart. She came from a dysfunctional sexually abusive family, and she had a real life story to tell. Her husband was verbally abusive and controlling, and would not let her be who she was. All fingers pointed to me as being the reason for her having to "self medicate". Any ignorant soul would fall for her act. Anyone who had not experienced a manipulative alcoholic, and did not have a program to follow, such as Al-Anon or AA, would bend over backwards to try and save her. And she knew it, and played the part as only a seasoned actress could do. Every few days Lisa would get the call to get tested. With the freedom of not having to work, she was able to fulfill the court's requirement. She had been coached well by her lawyer that if she wanted to regain control of her children and not be removed from the house then she would have to abide by the rules and not get caught drinking. In the end it would play to her advantage when we went back to court in the fall.

But I knew in my gut something "fishy" was going on. Something did not feel right, so I began to look around the house to see if there was anything out of the ordinary that might shed some light as to what was really going on. There was no way that she could keep herself from drinking, especially with her track record. While looking in the mudroom where the washing machine and dryer were located, I removed some of the cleaning products that were kept up in the shelves. I discovered a margarine container that looked out of place just behind the bottles that I had removed. I opened the top and found a strange yellowy liquid. It appeared like urine, but did not have a pungent smell to it. I thought I should get a second opinion, so I walked over to John and Lynne's house to see what they thought. I arrived at the back door and was met by Lynne. John was not home, so I decided I would show her the contents. She took one look at it and said, "Oh, Tom that isn't anything".

I felt dejected, and I did not wait around for any further discussion. As I was walking back to my house, I dumped the urine like substance on the ground. I thought if Lynne thought it was nothing, then how could I convince the court. I would have to get the liquid tested, and even then it would look as though I was tampering with evidence. But part of me did believe that I had blown my chance to get Lisa out of the house to get the help she required, and to gain full future control over my kids. The other thought I had was the relief I would not have to battle in court to prove the truth once again. I was already sick of the fight, and we had only just begun. I did call my attorney to tell her what I had found and that I had dumped it.

She was very upset. "Tom," she said, "that was evidence we could have used!"

I felt badly, but there was nothing I could do unless I found some more evidence. My antennae was up at all times, but Lisa was very clever. Surely she would have found that her important container was missing and would have to find a new way to hide her ill-gotten urine. My question was who was supplying this urine? Or was she saving her own clean urine when she was sober for a long enough period of time? She had too many friends who would bail her out knowing the bitter outcome that would be inflicted upon her.

Lisa and I did not say very much to each other. Living in the same house and knowing that the end of our marriage was looming was very bizarre. I still could not understand the rationale behind the court's decision. It was like water torture slowing driving me crazy. It did not seem to bother Lisa, because nothing had changed for her. She still did not have to go to work, and she was home all day to do whatever she pleased. I went to work each day worrying about what was happening back at home, and I did not have a backup plan to keep an eye on Lisa's behavior. She still had full access to our finances, and the Internet where she could torture me by her continuous buying habits and ruining our credit. The only relief was knowing that at some point in the future our marriage would be over and my mental and financial sanity would finally be protected.

When I arrived home from work I would play with the kids before dinner, eat as a family, and then lie down with the kids in between their beds telling silly stories and laughing a lot. Lisa would appear in the doorway looking disapprovingly at me thinking that I was acting immaturely around the kids. After she would go to our bedroom to sleep by herself, I would soon fall asleep in between Andrew and Krista's beds. At one point Lisa and I did talk of stopping the divorce, but even as attractive as that sounded, I knew that I would be giving in to the disease, and that her dangerous drinking would resume, and I would end up just as I was or worse. I was done, and so was our marriage.

BUSINESS TRIP

I had applied for the Northwestern Mutual Community Service Award back in March of 2002 hoping that I would win the covenant $10,000 grant for my 501(C)(3) environmental cleanup organization. With a lot of written support by my boss and board members I received the letter in June that my organization had won. I was thrilled. It meant not only a huge infusion of money to my event, but also a chance to go to the home office in Milwaukee and to be recognized on stage for all of my hard work in front of 10,000 of my peers. I was so excited, but at the same time nervous, because I had to figure out what to do with my three kids. Do I take them with me or do I leave them behind with Lisa? I had a one-year-old, which would make it almost impossible to go anywhere there at the meeting.

My mother knew of my plight and had already figured that she would take the children, and my father would accompany me on this trip. I felt very uncomfortable and sad, because I wanted my family there with me to see me on stage receiving this amazing award for all the hard work I had done over the past five years. But logistically it would not work. My big concern was how this would not only affect my kids, but how angry Lisa would be that I did not trust her enough to look after them. It almost felt like I was antagonizing her, even though she did not have custody of our children. The last thing I wanted was for her to invite her mother down to look after them with her, and at the same time bad mouth me while I was away. I knew that there would be repercussions, and any hope of our reconciling would be locked away for good. I felt like I was jumping out of my skin, and I told my parents how uneasy I felt, but they insisted it was best for their grandchildren, and I could not disagree.

So the tickets were purchased and the hotel reservations were made. My boss even had a cookout at our agency in honor of my achievement. Once again I was a little sad that my wife and kids were not able to be there. I was focused on my pain and loss of my marriage that I felt very out of sorts, but I had to keep moving forward. Andrew, Krista, Robert, and I drove to Mattapoisett to take a few days to enjoy the July 4th holiday. My parents and my brother John were there also. I felt very happy to be with everyone, and the kids had fun swimming and being with their cousins. I went to a local pub with John to have a beer and just talk. He seemed very relieved that things were moving forward and that my children were safe. I could not help but wonder what Lisa was doing at our house alone. Was she drinking or spending my money or seeing someone? For the first time I did not feel like I had any control over her actions, but at the same time I never did! I kept hoping that something would change inside her, and that she would miss the kids so much that she would do anything to change her behavior.

When we arrived home from our mini vacation, it appeared nothing had changed. She looked the same, and acted the same aloof way she had a few days earlier. I did not want to tell her my plans of having my parents look after our kids, but I knew I had to. If I did not do this, then when we went to court, her lawyer could prove to the judge that she was a fully responsible parent and should have custody of her children. This was both for show and safety, but I could not help feeling sad for my kids and what they were losing.

Lisa was not happy when I told her, and she said that her mother would be happy to come down and help out. I told her that I did not want Leslie anywhere near our home because of her antagonizing behavior. I told the kids that they would be staying with their grandparents for four days. Andrew could not understand why he had to leave his own home since his mother would be there. I told him it was for his own safety, but that did not sit well in his head.

The day came when I was to leave, and so I dropped the kids off, and took the bus to the airport with my dad. When we arrived in Milwaukee I felt a very strong pull to go back home to be with my family, but I had to fight the overwhelming fatherly urge to be with them. I told my father I was very frightened as to what was coming in the months ahead. He hugged me, but knew we all had to stay the course.

I had signed up for the "Roots and Wings" 10K road race to have something to focus on while in Milwaukee. I had never run more than four miles, but I thought how hard could it be? The morning of the race it was well over 90 degrees and very humid. There were actually two parts to the race—a 5K for novice racers and the 10K for the more die-hard racers. My manliness got the better of me, for when I had the choice to go right for the 5K or straight for the 10K, I chose the latter. I did not realize just how difficult this extra mileage would be especially in the driving heat and humidity. I did finish the race, but found no matter how hard I tried I could not cool down. Even after the cool mist showers that they had set up, and plenty of water to drink, I knew I was in trouble. My father and I went to the evening garden party held at the Milwaukee Zoo, and I was still having heat-stroke like symptoms. My dad was concerned, but I knew if I could just get out of the heat and stay in the air-conditioned hotel I would recover. The next day I felt much better and knew that would be my last long distance road race. By the time I was on stage with the 20 other CSA winners the next day I felt much better. After all that I had endured, it felt great to receive such positive recognition from such an amazing organization. I had called home to check on how things were going with my kids, and my mother was thrilled to have them. She handed the phone to Andrew and he said how much he missed being in his own home. I felt very guilty, and told him it would just be a few more days. My father overheard our conversation and was not happy that he heard guilt coming out of my mouth. After I hung up the phone, he said that I had to be strong at all times especially in front of the children. I knew he was right, but I still felt as though I had done something terribly wrong and my kids were suffering from my actions. The disease of alcoholism was screaming in my head.

THE NEXT PHASE—GAL ∼

I was back home after four days in Milwaukee being honored for my efforts in leading my environmental cleanup group. I was very happy to have all those accolades thrust upon me. Winning a $10,000 grant was a huge financial boost to my organization GreenUp Day, because it meant I received a great deal of recognition and press, as well as money to buy the t-shirts, work gloves, and trash bags that were vital in picking up tons of trash around Framingham. But I was home now to face an uphill battle. I was so happy to pick up my kids. They had not been happy being away from both their mother and me. They could not really understand why they could not just live with mommy while I was away. I knew that we had to build a case against Lisa and her alcoholism. If I trusted her enough to take care of the kids, then why was I seeking full custody?

That night Lisa suggested that we should try counseling again to figure all this out

"All you will do is manipulate another psychologist," I immediately said "That is out of the question. If you go away to Serenity House, then I will put a stop to this divorce."

"No," she said.

It would have been easy to agree to meet with another professional, but as history proved, she used them to continue her drinking. This was totally unacceptable to me. My entire family had been through too much, and I was not going to go through countless sleepless nights walking the streets of Framingham trying to figure out my next move. I had made it. Now it was time to see this thing through. Every other day Lisa received a phone call from the court telling her to go to Connections to be urine tested. She did as she was told, and easily passed each one whether or not she was cheating with someone else's pee. A few times I was tempted just to take her down to the police station to have her follicle tested, but she never appeared quite wobbly enough for me to take this kind of action. I wish that this type of testing would have been the norm, but it was not, so I had to wait for something big to appear. It never did.

Now that it was late in July, it was time to move this ordeal along. My lawyer said that I had to make an appointment with, our GAL, and give him my statement. I thought that if he were as open-minded as my lawyer had said, then this part would be easy. I would finally have someone outside my family on my side to protect my children. I called and made an appointment to go to his Boston office the following day. When I met him he appeared to be an older gentleman in his early 60's. He was very no nonsense and got right to the point. I felt like he was almost reading my rights, telling me that anything I said was going to be used in court and that he would not tolerate my trying to manipulate him in any way. I felt that telling the truth would be adequate, and that I did not have to worry about manipulating anyone. He told me that he was representing my children for the court and would do his best to get an accurate picture of what was best for them. He then told me to begin my account of what has happened to bring us to this point of separation. I began by saying that I would not even be here if Lisa had decided to get the help that she needed. He replied, "You know there are many ways to help her." I looked at him kind of stunned thinking, does this guy understand what we have been put through with this lying alcoholic? That was the first moment when I did not feel right about this guy.

I told him as much as I knew from the early days of our marriage when we visited my brother Will in Houston where she drank a bottle of Jack Daniels to the present of her most recent DUI. I tried not to embellish anything but the truth needed no embellishing. I could not quite figure this guy out, so I had to tell the truth and hope he would understand. After an hour he said it was time to rap things up, and that I should make an appointment with his secretary for the following week. Lisa was going to meet with him later in the week. I was very worried that she would lie, and he would buy into her story. I did not feel that he cared for me much, and with Lisa's charm she had already won over many unsuspecting professionals. He was supposed to be one of the best GAL's in the state. I truly hoped he lived up to the hype.

KEEP GOING

It was very weird living with Lisa in the same house while we were each jockeying for dominance over the other. I knew she would do anything to win, because losing meant the end of being a mother as she knew it. I was trying to force her into making the right decision for our family and our marriage. I naively believed that if the court would box her into a corner, then she would have to get help for her alcoholism. There were many flaws in my thinking. In reality, I had no control over the outcome, and if I lost, then my word as a father and a husband would change dramatically. In fact, it already had. What once was a parental unit, was now fractured and emotionless. The way things had become was not healthy for our children. All they saw was their parents who showed no love for each other. I was heartbroken that it had come to this. This is not what I had hoped, nor did I want this to continue, but I had to see it through.

TROJANS

The real truth was that everyone had taken sides. My family saw me as the victim of a crazed alcoholic. Lisa's side saw her as the victim of an abusive husband who was not supportive of her so-called sobriety. I rarely raised my voice to her nor did I ever hurt her physically, but I was abusive because I forced her to keep going to detox when she relapsed. I felt as though I was in one of those episodes of "The Twilight Zone" where I could see things clearly, but no one else could. The more I fought for justice, the deeper I dug my hole into despair. The world seemed upside down, and there was nothing I could do about it, except keep trying, in futile attempts, to change the minds of people who had the final decision of what was to come.

At one of the meetings with , our assigned GAL, I was asked to bring the kids with me to be observed how they interacted with each other. The meeting seemed to go well. The kids were well behaved and snuggled with me as the GAL asked his questions. At one point Andrew asked what was the percentage of parents getting back together?

"About 25%," he replied.

It was a matter-of-fact answer that did not give any of us much hope. I hoped that this meeting would prove that the kids were very happy to be with their dad, and that this would have no negative effect of Lisa's relationship with the kids. They loved her and she loved them, and that was all that mattered.

I hated to have the kids put in the middle of this divorce. I was not trying to have them pick which parent they loved more or even who they wanted to live with. My only goal was to have Lisa off of alcohol and to be a responsible parent, and of course save our ruined marriage. Lisa did go with the kids to see the GAL a few days later, and I learned nothing of what had transpired. All I knew was that she answered his questions and that the kids snuggled in with her just as they had with me. The GAL would only have our testimony, and the observance of how three children adored their parents, to make his final decision.

One day I came across a box of Trojans that I had kept stored in my bureau drawer and that I had forgotten about. I had my vasectomy a year earlier, and had kept the box just in case. For what I do not know, but I was surprised when I came across them and yelled to Lisa, "Look what I found!"

She came up to our bedroom and said, "I'll take care of that." I naively thought she was going to throw them out. What I did not realize that in her devious mind, she would use them to disparage my reputation with the GAL. At her next one-on-one meeting with Len Worman she told him that she had found an opened Trojan wrapper in my wallet. So of course this painted me as a cad in the eyes of the decision maker.

What made me angry was the fact that he never questioned her about what she had brought him. He did not let on that he knew something about me that would be used against me in his final report. Len Worman had said that he would not tolerate any manipulation of the court, and yet that is exactly what she was doing. I truly believed that all the experts would see right through her lies, but instead they fell prey to her made-up stories. I thought that staying with the truth was the only way to play fairly with these so-called experts, and I was not about to lie my way through the court system.

The system I found was stacked against the truth, and used it to enable the victim. This was the only way that it could afford to keep from paying for the thousands of people with addictions. The court system is built on enabling those less fortunate to survive, but in reality it does just the opposite. It costs families their wealth and most often their livelihood, and then breaks them apart and keeps them that way. If the truth shall set you free, then I was well on my way. I may not like the outcome, but I was on a one-way train out of my marriage, and I could see the end of the line.

During my next meeting with the GAL I was asked about the night I had to call the police to keep Lisa from taking the children to her mother's. I got very excited and said that she had lied to the police six times when questioned about her drinking. Without thinking I had embellished what I knew to make my point, but in the eyes of Len Worman I was stretching the truth to manipulate the court in my favor. He said that in the police report Lisa had only lied to them once. At that point I knew that my excitement had gotten me in trouble, and given him ammunition to take me down. I was no longer just a philanderer, but a liar too. I tried to recover by saying that I was sorry that I might have embellished the truth. He told me to go to the Framingham Police Department and request to see the report from the police officer that night. I knew that this was going to lead me nowhere, and that it would just prove his point. I had also told him that the judge had called Lisa "a raging alcoholic". He asked me, "Are you sure the judge made that statement?" I said, "Absolutely", but in the court documents there was no mention of it by the court stenographer. Once again I looked foolish, and felt demoralized. After leaving his office I called my lawyer to say that I had blown it. She tried to calm me down, and told me not to worry. I was worried, very worried.

WAITING GAME

It appeared Lisa was in complete control over the court system. She had the GAL right where she wanted him, just as she had snowed the case workers at Connections in believing she was ok. The GAL believed her stories and not mine. She had remained calm and cool, and I had been truthful and emotional, which made me appear out of control and abusive. Len Worman had looked for an excuse to find something negative about me, and he had found it. Now that all the meetings with him were complete, all I could do was wait.

The most important court date of my life and my family's life was scheduled for November 1st, the day after Halloween.

That meant more weeks of receiving a cold shoulder from Lisa. Except for one night while I was lying in the bed next to Andrew, Lisa came into the room and seductively whispered in my ear to come into her room for the night. I was astonished that she would ask me, but I also knew that it meant that she must be intoxicated, because that was when she would get horny and let her guard down. Just as I was about to respond, Krista came into the room saying that she wanted to sleep with momma tonight. I knew that fate had stepped in just in time, because if I had acted upon my sexual needs that it would derail all that was supposed to happen. I truly believe that my angels in the universe were looking out for me and through my daughter stepped in at just the right moment.

TRYING TO FIND REASON

I was truly hoping that after Len Worman had read the police report on Lisa, as well as my testimony that he would do what was best to keep our kids safe, and that was to give me full custody of them. That would force Lisa's hand to having to go to Serenity House and stop fooling herself. I truly felt my actions were honorable, and that in the end Lisa would beat her demons, but this was all my conjured-up fantasy. Lisa had no intention of losing control of her kids. The unknown was too scary, and the thought of not being able to drink any more was out of the question. I thought if she did not have the will to quit drinking and face her past, then I was the guy to help her. In the end I learned I was powerless over this dreaded disease, and that the only thing I could do was allow my Higher Power to take over and do what was right. I had false control, and I had done everything I could do. Now it was up to a GAL and a kangaroo court to decide the fate of my broken family. In all of this, Lisa had shown no signs of trying to get well, so what was I thinking? Desperate times means taking desperate measures, but I was sailing my ship without a rudder, and my compass did not know where true north was located. So I had to put all my faith in people that I did not trust, and could not figure out, and worse I was paying a lot of money for an outcome that I probably was not going to like. I thought that if the GAL report did not go in my favor, then I could reason with Lisa to forget the whole mess, and stay together as a family, no matter how crazy this sounded in my head.

TRICK OR TREAT

I took Andrew and Krista out trick or treating across the street from where my parents live and had fun watching them go door to door asking for candy and saying thank you each time. But as I was walking, I could not help but think what I was about to walk into the next day. After we were all done, we walked in to see my mom and dad at their house to say goodby for the night. I went in for some moral support. Nothing felt right, and I felt totally out of control of my situation. I could not believe that tomorrow was the day that my entire life was going to change if Len Worman's report was not in my favor. All the time and money wasted trying to force my wife into treatment was just unimaginable. At the same time I just wanted the insanity to be over and to get on with my life.

The day finally arrived. I met my lawyer in the Cambridge courthouse and hoped that she could give me some hope and encouragement, but there was not a whole lot she could do or say. It all came down to the last page of the GAL's report. A few minutes later Lisa and her lawyer arrived. I heard her lawyer say to Lisa that if the report did not go in their favor that they would appeal. That gave me a little hope that her lawyer did not think it was going to go the way they had planned.

Len Worman came walking into the main open meeting area of the courthouse carrying a thick report. He walked up to us, and without looking me in the eye said in a sarcastic manner to Rebecca, "I hope this is what you wanted".

I thought that was a weird thing to say. I was taken aback and thought that this was not going to go in my favor. As we began reading the first page of the report in the very first paragraph it stated how I believed the judge was an alcoholic, and that I believed she should be removed from the bench! Lisa had taken out of context what I had said months earlier and used those words against me. My lawyer was shocked that the GAL would write something so farfetched and devastating to our side on the very first page!

Later that day she got on the phone with him and pleaded for him to redact those words from the report. Out of respect for her he did. I felt ashamed that I had underestimated Lisa's sense of morality and fair play, and the truth for that matter. We skimmed most of the report to go right to the final page to find out what the recommendation was for us. His final summation was that both Lisa and I have joint legal and physical custody of the children. Lisa had beaten the system, and the system had beaten me. She now would have the kids back, and she did not have to ask my permission for anything. I was devastated, and there was nothing I could do to change the results. My worst fears had become reality. I called my brother to give him the news. There was a very long pause at the other end, and then he said, "Well it looks like they all stick together don't they?"

Why had I gone through all this hell? I thought my lawyer was supposed to protect me and my kids. Getting angry really was not going to help my situation, but I did feel like a victim. The first words spoken by Lisa's attorney to me were, "You're going to have to find another place to live."

At that point I felt, for the first time, that I had officially lost. I was an outcast from my own house, and I felt like my family had been pulled apart. I had no idea what I was going to do at this point. I felt that my parents and my minister and my lawyer were all to blame for not protecting me from what could have happened and which did happen. In my gut I knew that this was the only course that could have been taken, but I was just so angry. I was very fearful of the unknown. I did not know where I was going to end up, and worse that nothing had changed. Lisa was now free to drink, even though she was still being tested for alcohol. She had access to our finances, and she could go on behaving like a raving alcoholic around the kids. The courts had allowed her bad behavior to continue, and I was left holding the shattered pieces of what was left of my family. And what did joint legal and physical custody really mean? Why was I asked to leave the house that I was paying for, and then be expected to find another place to pay for? This was obscene, unfair, and ridiculous!

HER UPPER HAND

After we arrived home, I felt a little relief that I was allowed in the house. She asked me when I was planning on leaving, but I did not have an answer. I was not prepared or willing to go anywhere at this point. In fact a few days later I decided to go to the one person that had the power to change the course of my hell—the one person who had caused it. I suggested that we go to lunch to discuss our family's future. She agreed. At the restaurant I told her that this whole mess was for one reason, and that was to help her stop her drinking. It had nothing to do with not wanting to be married or splitting our family apart. I also said that we could not afford to have two households, and that it would not be fair to the kids. I suggested that we stay living together for now in separate rooms, and that I would stop the divorce proceedings as well as the alcohol testing.

I waited for an answer, but she did not really say anything. She knew she had me and had the upper hand. I knew it too. She gave me nothing, which made me very uneasy, but I thought if I made this drastic move, then she might have a change of heart and want to stay married. The next day I called my lawyer to tell her to stop the divorce proceedings, as well as the alcohol testing. She said that was a very bad idea and that it would only weaken my position. I said that I had made my decision, and that nothing else had worked up to this point. She said that the court had been very favorable in their ruling. I did not believe this to be true, and at this point I did not know who to believe or who was right or whether was I wrong. I had to take matters into my own hands. At least now I would feel that I had taken back some of my control, and let everyone else go to hell.

So she reluctantly wrote a letter asking the court to cancel the divorce proceedings as well as the alcohol testing. I then told Lisa. Once again she said basically nothing. She gave me no sense of well being, and at that point I knew I was playing right into her hands. Now she could do whatever she wanted, which was no different except now she had no fear of being caught. The inconvenience had been removed, and now she only had one more obstacle to get me out of the house, and that was going to happen sooner rather than later. I called my mother to let her know of my decision. She then told my father who then called my psychologist to give him the news that I was trying to reconcile with Lisa. None of them were happy with my decision, because they knew how crafty she was, and that nothing good could come out of this.

A few weeks went by with no discussion about reconciliation , in fact Lisa was just as aloof from me as ever. If she wanted to stay together she certainly had made no moves towards this outcome. I knew at that point that I had made the wrong decision, and that I had to make some kind of statement. I thought that if I took my clothes out of our closet and moved them to my parent's house that she would see what it would be like with me out of the house, and with her having to handle all the responsibilities of raising three children by herself. So I grabbed my clothes while Lisa was up in our room, and told her I was moving to my parent's for a little while until we could sort things out. She said nothing.

I drove to my parents, and told them I was going to move into the guest room for a little while. There really was no room in the closet for my suits, so I called my attorney to tell her that the divorce was once again on.

"Fine," she said, "but this may have hurt your position, but it is the right thing to do."

I then asked my father about the possibility of moving into Vernon House. It had been a nursing home, but had closed down the year before due to the lack of old ladies dying out. He was the acting president. I said that I could be the caretaker while the board decided what to do with the place. He said that he would ask. He did, and they agreed. My next stop was going to be moving into a fully furnished 22 room nursing home.

ALTITUDE SICKNESS ∾

During Christmas time, my brother Will came up from Houston Texas to visit the family. He had also made plans to go with his kids to Stowe Vermont for a few days and invited our parents to come along. I asked if I could come up with

Andrew, because I would like him to experience the largest mountain in Vermont. Will said sure. I needed to get away for a few days to clear my head, and really think all this through before I moved out.

Once we were up at the condo directly across from the ski resort, we unpacked and then had a nice dinner. Unfortunately I ate the lamb which gave me terrible gas most of the night. My son and nephew were not happy sleeping in the same room as me! After dinner I sat down with my parents around the dining table to discuss my options. Will popped his head around the corner and looked at me in a very disapproving way, as if I were doing something mean to my parents.

I knew this conversation was going to go nowhere, so I decided to get up and leave the room.

I was very confused as to why I was made to feel guilty about getting my family's opinion about something that was going to affect everyone, especially my kids! I guess Will just felt that what was done was done, and that it was time to get on with my life and begin the healing process. It felt so wrong, but he was right.

I felt very alone, and sad. The next day Andrew and I were skiing down The National which is a black diamond trail. The skiing did not last long, because as I stopped to look at a very steep part of the trail. Andrew did not take heed and zoomed down hitting two moguls and then wiping out face first. I slowly skied towards him. He was not happy, and said that he had had enough. I was not happy that our day of skiing was over, and my brother was waiting at the top of the mountain for us. There was no way to contact him, because we did not have our cell phones with us. So we slogged back to the condo in our ski boots cursing every step we took on the pavement. We decided to go home the next day, and I would soon be back in our house counting down the days before I would leave to start my new life in a nursing home.

When we returned, Lisa kept asking when I was going to be leaving. I kept thinking why am I leaving? You are the one with the drinking problem! How am I going to keep my kids safe? If my kids had been in danger while I was living there, who would keep a watchful eye? The fox was soon going to be left totally alone in the hen house, and I felt that I was being pushed out by everyone. I needed someone to step in and save me and my kids from this insanity, but it seemed like there was no one around. I tried one last time to meet with my minister. I asked why was this happening to me? She just looked at me and said, "Tom, you have to be stronger than this. You will get through it." I went to my psychologist to ask him for some advice. He said, "You messed up. You trusted us!" I think he was being sarcastic, because he knew all the pain Lisa had put me and the kids through. He knew there was no other way out, but to get out and save myself and he too was right.

TAROT CARDS

One day while I was driving home on Route 9, I saw a sign that read "Tarot Cards Read". I decided to pull in to have my cards read for no other reason than to get some answers and possibly some much needed guidance. As I walked in the Goth-looking woman said that she was not supposed to be in today. It was just by chance she was in. During my reading she spoke of my wife and said that she was like a Hoover Vacuum Cleaner sucking my soul out of me and that it was time that I moved away from her. I had not told her anything about my situation. I was glad that she had validated my actions. That was all I needed from her, so I left.

I stalled as long as I could before beginning to move my

clothes to Vernon House. The house was old and so was the plumbing. There was no hot water, so I was not about to move in if I could not take a hot shower in the middle of winter! After another weeklong delay, the house was ready for me to move in. I was met by one of the board of directors to go over the alarm system and what my duties of the house were going to be. Pretty much I could do as I wished, as long as I turned the alarm back on when I left the house. There was also an antiquated sprinkler system that when the pressure was too low I would have to go down into the creepy basement and turn on the loud generator to fill the pressure back up. I was hoping I would never have to do that in the middle of the night. The house was scary enough with me conjuring up thoughts of ghosts from past residents hovering around me.

My lowest point in my life hit me between the eyes as I sat on the edge of my single bed in room 1A on the first floor of a nursing home. I thought what just happened to me? At one point I was the happiest man alive being the father of three kids, married and a successful businessman, paying my bills on time and knowing exactly who I was. Now, I was so far out of my comfort zone I nearly wanted to jump out of my skin. I did not know what to do with myself. My whole world revolved around being with my kids and playing with them and helping them with their homework. How did I go from 100% custody to looking in from the outside of my house? I felt like nothing, that I was just a piece of useless trash. And then when I thought that nothing worse could happen to me, the sprinkler's warning bell went off at two in the morning. I had to get up from a sound sleep, turn on all the lights that I could find and go into the furthest part of the musty basement and turn on the loud generator! The only thing that I could control was how I was going to deal with my new situation without falling completely apart.

I decided I would keep busy with cleaning up Vernon house by vacuuming all the rooms, and making sure that all the windows were completely closed to keep the cost of the oil down for the owners, and because I lived so close to our house, I would go over as much as possible. Lisa was amenable to allow me to keep my practice electronic drum set in the old room, so that I could have a quiet place to play. It was a very weird situation, because she did allow me in the house a lot to see the kids. The main reason she wanted me out was so that she could continue to do what she wanted to do without any interference from me. I was still hoping that we would get back together, even though it would make no sense since neither of us trusted the other. Because she was still living in the house, and I was paying the mortgage, my child support was cut in half for the time being. I was amazed that I could put on a professional face in spite of the mental trauma I had been through. I continued to go to Al-Anon to get positive support from my group members, and I saw my therapist. I remember saying to him, "I guess my life is over. I will never meet anyone again and find love." He just laughed and said, "We'll see how long that lasts!" I knew he was right, but I needed to feel sorry for myself. I did not feel like anyone could feel what I was going through unless they were in my shoes, and at the same time I did not want anyone else to feel that pain that I was feeling. Now for the first time in 20 years I had time to really think, and for the first time the focus was all on me and not on my alcoholic wife. I was free.

VERNON HOUSE

Now that I was out of the marital home, the arrangement was that I had the kids on Wednesday nights and from Friday to Sunday night. It felt very strange that I was not seeing them every day. It again felt as though I was being punished for taking any kind of action against my wife. But the kids and I made the most of it with playing hide and go seek, wheelchair races, and soccer in the big room on the third floor. The kids slept in the room next to mine, and we all either made our meals in the big industrial kitchen or walked up the street to Centre Pizza to buy our grinders. We all made our time in Vernon House a new adventure, but I still in the back of my mind hoped that this would all wind up righting itself and Lisa and I would be back together in our house. Whenever Lisa came by to pick up the kids she always seemed annoyed to see me. I was not sure if she was mad that I had put her into her new position and responsibilities or was she fighting her urge to drink? I just felt as though the longer I was out of the house the less chance we would get back together.

A few weeks later I met a beautiful woman, and we began to date. She was newly separated also with three kids the same ages as mine. We kept our dating secret so not to rock the boat with our spouses. Before anything became too serious, I decided to speak to Lisa about getting back together. As we sat down together on the edge of Andrew's bed in our house I asked her, "Is there any chance that you will consider getting back together with me? I am considering going into a new relationship, but I won't if you want me back."

She did not hesitate for a moment and replied, "No, I don't love you anymore."

I asked again, "Are you absolutely sure?"

She said yes that she was sure. So with that I knew it was officially over, and that I had given everything I possibly could to make our marriage work and to try to bring it back from the ashes. I walked out of the house again feeling very sad. I truly did want our marriage to have worked, but with her not trusting me, and me not willing to go back to the way it was, it was time to move on with the next chapter of my life.

HARSH REALITY

Now, looking back, I learned so much from my alcoholic situation. The sense of control that I thought I had from the very beginning was all an illusion. The alcoholic has their own set of rules, and none of it fits into the world of reality. Their only concern, if not in a 12 step program, is after the pain returns how am I going to drink again. I truly believed that once I could just get through and offer my well-intentioned advice, that she would see the light and get well. I had no idea what I was up against. I thought I was getting ahead of the disease by going to professionals in the mental health substance abuse world, but amazingly, unless they are going to a 12 step program themselves, then they too are at the mercy of the alcoholic. I found that with all the great advice I received, some of it actually helped my problem. But what I also learned was to take what you need and leave the rest. Until someone has experienced an alcoholic in action and has been subjected to crazy behavior, then there is nothing one can do to fix them. The only person you can fix is yourself, and in this particular situation the only true help is through the Al Anon and AA 12 step programs. There are no winners or losers, and with that said I had to let my ego go, and just surrender to the disease. Once I stopped fighting the invisible foe, I was able to let the universe take over and guide me through the morass of emotions.

    I also realized that we have the best legal system in the world, but at the same time it is greatly flawed. There are so many cases like mine that there is just not enough time to truly see the reality for what it is, and that bias plays a big part in it. The outcome of my case was really never in doubt in my mind, because I had already seen too much of the way the system enables the sick person. Tough Love would be the best way to help the alcoholic, but to do it the right way would cost too much money. I believe that bringing in the legal system has to be the last resort after using up all other resources. In the end it was my decision and mine alone that I took to protect my family. Now, looking back, it has taken me years to understand all that I have been through and to accept the decisions that I made. What I did discover that through all of this I found the real me and that I am a lot stronger than I realized.